The Panama Canal:
Heart of America's Security

Frontispiece: Miraflores lake, the bottleneck Pedro Miguel locks, located squarely across the south end of Gaillard cut, looking northward. The problem of this dangerous bottleneck would be solved in the Terminal Lake-Third Locks Plan by the elimination of these locks.

The Panama Canal:
Heart of America's Security

by

Jon P. Speller

Robert Speller & Sons, Publishers, Inc.
New York, New York 10010

Library of Congress Catalog Card No. 72-178828
ISBN O-8315-0119-7

First Edition

Printed in the United States of America

Robert Speller & Sons, Publishers, Inc.
New York, New York 10010

To the builders, operators and defenders of the Panama Canal.

TABLE OF CONTENTS

LIST OF ILLUSTRATIONS

INTRODUCTION

The purpose of this book is to clarify and simplify the issues revolving around the Panama Canal. No great issue has been subject to such confusion as has this one. Congressman Daniel J. Flood, Senator Strom Thurmond and many of their colleagues have incessantly revealed the truth concerning the Panama Canal issue. But advocates of a costly new sea-level canal and advocates of our surrendering our attributes of sovereignty over the Canal Zone have persisted in their attempts to cloud the issues.

As a result, the much-needed modernization of the Canal has been delayed. It is our hope that this book will cut through the fog of confusion and help the passage of those bills related to the improvement of the canal — bills which have been thoroughly studied and prepared. If it can serve to remove the current impedimenta to their passage it can represent, in my belief, a contribution to the future security of ourselves, our children and future generations of Americans.

New York   Jon P. Speller

The Panama Canal:
Heart of America's Security

Chapter One

Basic Principles of U. S. Panama Canal Policy

No territorial possession of the United States is of greater strategic importance than the Canal Zone. No property of the United States is of greater economic importance than the Panama Canal. These two fundamental considerations have determined the principles on which U. S. Panama Canal policy, from its inception, has been based.

The basic principles of U. S. Panama Canal policy have evolved, and still revolve, around three cardinal issues:

1. United States sovereignty over the territory on which the Isthmian Canal is constructed
2. The most appropriate *site* for an Isthmian Canal
3. The most appropriate *type* of Isthmian Canal

The first principle demands United States sovereignty over Isthmian Canal territory in order to assure that interoceanic transit between the Atlantic and Pacific Ocean is permanently secure to world commerce in time of peace and to assure that interoceanic transit is denied to our enemies in time of war. Exclusive United States sovereignty over the Canal Zone became a basic principle of U. S. Panama Canal policy. For this reason United States sovereignty must be maintained unimpaired.

1

Without the cession of sovereignty to the United States the Panama Canal would never have been built. Without the continued United States sovereignty over the Canal Zone the Canal would in all probability have long since ceased to be operational. Without United States sovereignty the future of the Canal would be highly problematical.

This principle does not permit a concept of cession of sovereignty to another nation, nor a "joint sovereignty" with another nation, nor an internationalization of the Canal. Each of these alternatives poses the same problem. Governments and regimes change. Even the most friendly regime of a most friendly nation can change in composition and goals through events in its internal affairs which are not within our jurisdiction. This is also true of international organizations and cliques therein. The interests of our global commerce could, under certain circumstances, suffer drastically from a deliberate policy of another nation or an international organization possessing total or partial sovereignty over the Isthmian Canal. If that eventuality should arise, with United States sovereignty lost, such a policy of another nation or an international organization could be implemented with legal impunity. It should not be suggested from this inference that the United States would thereby have abdicated its right to defend its national interests by force of arms. Any nation retains, regardless of international convention or mores, the right to take steps necessary for its own survival in the comity of nations. But why, when foresight and resolution make it unnecessary, should we ever have to exercise such an option?

Our sovereignty over the Canal Zone provides a full range of options. Much has been said of the military indefensibility of the present Panama Canal in the event of nuclear war. However, it has not been sufficiently stressed that the military elements determining this indefensibility would be largely applicable to any Isthmian Canal. The prime strategic consideration for the United States in the event of a global nuclear holocaust could not be to ensure an adequate defense of an Isthmian Canal. It would be to deny access to the Canal to the enemy and to nonbelligerents carrying materiale to the enemy. If the Canal were under the sovereignty of another nation or an international organization, under certain circumstances interoceanic transit for enemy vessels and trade by neutrals with the enemy via the Canal would be possible.

Under conditions of less than a world conflict, the danger is even greater. In the Cuba of 1960 the author heard from many the belief that the United States would never long tolerate an aggressive, unfriendly government in this hemisphere. Events have shown, especially in 1962, that considerations of our global policy can effectively handicap the United States from exercising a policy in its best interests in a local area, even one but ninety miles from our shores. It seems that we have had to tolerate, and continue to tolerate, the Castro dictatorship in Cuba. We cannot afford a replay of this situation with the Panama Canal at stake. The reader should keep in mind that our global posture is almost indispensably supported by transport through the Panama Canal. The logistics problem for our forces overseas which an even temporary loss of use of the Panama Canal would cause is staggering to contemplate. Vietnam war related traffic through the Canal is estimated to average four to five vessels per day.

Short of detrimental policies towards the United States, actions by an inimical nation or a nation benevolently neutral in favor of our opponents, domestic strife, anarchy or revolution within another nation possessing sovereignty over an Isthmian Canal could result in effectively closing the Canal.

A localized conflict between such a nation and a neighboring state could also produce the same result. Need an example other than that of the recent fate of the Suez Canal be cited? From June 1967 to the present the famed "life-line of Empire" has been closed. The crackle of firearms still echoes over the Suez Canal. Thousands of ships have been forced to make costly and time-consuming detours around the Cape of Good Hope.

The national security interests of the United States are best served by continued United States sovereignty over the Canal Zone. There are no conceivable engineering feats or defense systems which can approach this fact in significance for our national security. Indeed, certain engineering and defense system proposals could so impair our sovereign rights that, if enacted, alleged improvements would be accompanied by serious, probably irreparable, loss.

It should be noted that although talking about the present canal which we feel to be, with certain improvements, to be sufficient for current and forthcoming needs, we are not just referring to the Republic of Panama when discussing the aforementioned dangers. Each eventuality could be equally possible if there were a new canal through Colombia or Nicaragua.

The other two basic principles of U. S. Panama Canal policy, however, limit the practical scope to the present canal.

One of these principles concerns the *site* of the Isthmian Canal. Different sites — in Nicaragua, Mexico, Colombia and parts of Panama other than that ceded as the Canal Zone — have been suggested as possible alternative or additional canal routes. But of all possible routes that are suggested, the one encompassed by the Panama Canal is without peer. The present canal route is one practically dictated by nature. Other possible routes face natural obstacles — totally unnecessary natural obstacles. There is no reason to strive against nature when one can go along with nature. For example, on a map the distance traversing the Isthmus seems slight. Yet, it is not flat terrain. The topography provides challenges to tax man's ingenuity. The Continental Divide goes down the Isthmus, and, at only two points — in Panama and in Nicaragua — is the Divide less than six hundred feet high. All in all, the present route is by far the most practical. Each alternative route is characterized by massive natural, economic and political difficulties.

The third basic principle of U. S. Panama Canal policy concerns the type of an Isthmian Canal, i.e., whether the high-level-lake and lock or sea level type canal. This principle is the subject of renewed controversy. But this controversy is artificial. Serious analysis shows that the present high-level-lake and lock canal, with certain improvements, cannot be excelled in meeting the criteria upon which the choice of the type of Isthmian Canal must be predicated. The criteria, in essence, are based upon economic considerations and, above all, *navigational* suitability.

Of the two basic types of canal, the sea level canal is by far the most expensive. It would still require at least one lock facility. This is unavoidable because of the tidal differences between the Atlantic and the Pacific. As the Atlantic tidal range is approximately twenty-two inches as compared to the Pacific's twenty-two feet maximum, and the mean sea level of the Pacific Ocean is slightly higher than that of the Atlantic, the net flow is from the Pacific to the Atlantic. Perhaps the proponents of a new sea level canal have a solution to the problem — a latter-day King Canute who will command the Pacific Ocean to change its tide so that the lock would not be needed. Reason prescribes, however, that King Neptune will be no more heedful of a modern King Canute than he was of the historical one.

It is important to note that the Suez Canal — a sea level type of canal — can be blocked by the sinking of vessels in its channel. This can be accomplished by means of primitive weapons. This is no longer a theoretical possibility. It is a reality, and an Isthmian sea level canal would be just as vulnerable.

The Chicago Tribune* editorialized:

"An authoritative study in the *New Middle East,* a London periodical, concludes that there is no commercial future for the Suez Canal, which has been closed since the six day war in 1967. The development of giant tankers and ore carriers and the advent of containers for dry cargoes will make the Suez Canal non-competitive with other routes.

"A single tanker of 200,000 tons plying between British ports and the Persian Gulf can cut more than $1 a ton off the price of carrying the same quantity of oil via the canal route in the largest tankers (75,000 tons) that could transit the canal fully loaded in 1967.

"This experience proves that American shipping experts were right when they told the Johnson Administration there was no economic justification for a sea level canal in Panama. The present high-level lake-lock canal, with improvements nearing

---

* June 7, 1969

completion and others now contemplated, will be adequate for potential traffic well into the next century. Ships that are too large for the present canal would avoid a sea level canal because of the toll costs."

These economic points are valid, unless the American taxpayer is willing to subsidize canal traffic with artificially low rates. We do not need a White Elephant Isthmian Canal. We need a functioning canal suitable for current and projected needs.

Perhaps of most importance, even if located within the present Canal Zone, construction of a sea level canal would entail violations of our treaty arrangements with Panama, thus providing justification for the challenging of our sovereignty.

The present high-level-lake and lock Panama Canal, with certain major improvements incorporated in the Terminal Lake-Third Locks proposal developed during World War II as a result of war experience, provides the most economic and the navigationally superior type of canal for the Isthmus.

The Terminal Lake-Third Locks plan has been submitted to the Congress of the United States. A bill in the Senate, introduced by Senator Strom Thurmond (Republican, South Carolina), and a bill in the House of Representatives, introduced by Congressman Daniel J. Flood (Democrat, Pennsylvania), provide authorization for its implementation. These bills provide for all that is necessary to increase the capacity and improve the operations of the Panama Canal.

Arguments in favor of what these bills stand for are well stated in Resolution by the National Convention of the American Legion:

"WHEREAS, in 1903, the United States and the Republic of Panama entered into a treaty "to insure the construction of a ship canal across the Isthmus of Panama to connect the Atlantic and Pacific Oceans:" and

"WHEREAS, by that treaty, the Republic of Panama (for a lump-sum payment of ten million dollars in gold, plus an annuity now amounting to nearly two million dollars) granted to the United States in perpetuity the use, occupation and control of a zone of land and land under water for the construction, maintenance, operation, sanitation and protection of the canal, and granted to the United States all the rights, power, and authority, within the zone mentioned, "which the United States would possess and exercise if it were the sovereign of the territory within which said lands and waters are located, to the entire exclusion of the exercise by the Republic of Panama of any such sovereign rights, power or authority"; and

"WHEREAS, the Panama Canal now represents a total United States investment of nearly five billion dollars, and is a vital strategic asset to the United States for hemispheric defense and our own national security; and

"WHEREAS, the Panama Canal also is of great economic importance to the United States, inasmuch as 70 percent of traffic through the Canal either originates or terminates in U. S. ports, and Canal operations represent a net gain for U. S. balance-of-payments of more than 40 million dollars annually; and

"WHEREAS, The American Legion has consistently expressed its strong opposition to any weakening of the United States sovereign rights, power, and authority over the Panama Canal and the Canal Zone; now, therefore, be it

"RESOLVED: That The American Legion reaffirms its positions heretofore taken with regard to the Panama Canal and the Canal Zone, and opposes any new Canal treaties that would abrogate the essential provisions of the 1903 Treaty between the United States and the Republic of Panama; and

"FURTHER RESOLVED, That The American Legion urges both the House of Representatives and the Senate of the United States Congress to adopt a Joint Resolution expressing it to be the sense of the Congress and the Nation that the Government of the United States shall maintain and protect its sovereign rights in the Panama Canal Zone and its jurisdiction over the Panama Canal, and that the United States shall in no way forfeit, cede, or transfer any of these rights or jurisdiction to any other administration, government, or international organization; and

"FURTHER RESOLVED, That The American Legion

urges the Congress of the United States also to adopt legislation to provide for an increase in the capacity and for operational improvements of the existing Panama Canal in accord with the principles of the so-called 'Terminal Lakes-Third Locks Plan'."

It should be noted that the nearly two million dollars per annum paid to Panama by the United States is not entirely paid out of Panama Canal revenues. The sum of $430,000 is so charged (originally $250,000 per annum, it was increased, and rightfully so, when the United States devalued the dollar in 1934). The other $1,500,000 per annum is not charged to Canal revenues but to Department of State appropriations. It is thus a tribute to the oligarchs and juntas who play the game of "musical chairs" for power in Panama, land of endemic revolution.

The Terminal Lake-Third Locks Plan for modernization of the existing Panama Canal was approved by President Franklin D. Roosevelt. Its implementation was delayed by inertia and red herrings based upon unrealistic post-World War II hysteria over nuclear possibilities, possibilities which are not even relevant to the issue of an Isthmian Canal!

President Nixon, the Senate and the House could give no better service to the future serenity of the citizens of our Republic than by re-affirming the considered judgment on improving the Panama Canal reached by our World War II Commander-in-Chief.

Chapter Two

United States Sovereignty Over the Canal Zone

The Panama Canal would not be in existence today as a major artery of world commerce and an important factor in hemispheric defense if it were not for United States sovereignty over the Canal Zone. We would never have constructed the Canal, and we would never have maintained, improved and defended it, if sovereignty had not been granted us. The *sine qua non* of United States involvement in the Isthmian Canal was and is our absolute sovereignty over the territory concerned. This is an historical fact and a political reality.

Before one penny of U. S. funds was committed to the construction of an Isthmian Canal; before one step of commitment by the United States was made to Panama; indeed, even before the birth of the Republic of Panama, the United States officially stipulated that it demanded exclusive control, ownership and management of any Isthmian Canal before it would be willing to undertake any such project.

Under the first United States treaty with Panama, the Hay-Bunau-Varilla Treaty signed November 18, 1903, sovereign

9

powers, rights and authority over the Canal Zone were granted in perpetuity to the United States.

This treaty was ratified by the Republic of Panama on December 2, 1903. It came into effect upon the exchange of ratification in Washington on February 26, 1904.

The parts of the Hay-Bunau-Varilla Treaty concerning United States sovereignty are contained in Articles II and III:

"Article II: The Republic of Panama grants to the United States in perpetuity the use, occupation and control of a zone of land and land under water for the construction, maintenance, operation, sanitation and protection of said Canal of the width of ten miles extending to the distance of five miles on each side of the center line of the route of the Canal to be constructed. . . . with the proviso that the cities of Panama and Colon and the harbors adjacent to said cities. . . . shall not be included within this grant. . . .

"Article III: The Republic of Panama grants to the United States all the rights, power and authority within the zone mentioned and described in Article II of this agreement. . . . which the United States would possess and exercise if it were the sovereign. . . . to the entire exclusion of the exercise by the Republic of Panama of any such sovereign rights, power or authority."

These Articles are as much in effect today as they were the day the ratifications were exchanged. They are specific. They implicitly grant to the United States all sovereign rights to the Canal Zone.

The term of time for which the United States is granted such sovereignty is in perpetuity. What does that mean? Perpetually. Forever. As long as our flag shall wave as the symbol of a sovereign nation. . . .

The sovereign rights in the Canal Zone, with all of its accompanying power and authority, are ours to possess and exercise as if we were sovereign.

Further, these sovereign rights are vested in us by the treaty "to the *entire exclusion* of the exercise by the Republic of Panama of any such sovereign rights, power or authority."

Thus sovereignty over the Canal Zone passed hands from the Republic of Panama to the United States.

Under the Constitution of the United States the respective States have ceded certain powers to the Union, retaining all those powers to themselves which under the original Constitution or by amendment have not been ceded to the Federal Government.

The Republic of Panama similarly retains one such right, a so-called "titular sovereignty." This right is neither more nor less than a reversionary interest should the United States cease to exercise its rights over the Canal Zone.

Distinguished American statesmen, such as John Hay, William Howard Taft and Charles Evans Hughes have long since clarified its meaning. Congressman Daniel J. Flood, who has devoted many years of study to canal problems and who qualifies as a leading expert on the Panama Canal, records key factors of the history of the "titular sovereignty" concept:

"Secretary of Government Tomas Arias of Panama, one of the revolutionary junta of 1903, in a note dated May 25, 1904, addressed to Gov. George W. Davis of the Canal Zone stated:

'The Government of the Republic of Panama considers that upon the exchange of ratification of the treaty for opening the interoceanic canal across the Isthmus of Panama, its jurisdiction ceased over the zone.' Ratification of this treaty, it may be stated, were exchanged on February 26, 1904.

"In spite of this clear, unequivocal declaration, Secretary Arias later presented the 'sovereignty' question to the United States. In a comprehensive reply to the Panamanian Government on October 24, 1904, Secretary of State Hay asserted that 'the great object to be accomplished by the treaty is to enable the United States to construct the canal by the expenditure of public funds of the United States — funds created by the collection of taxes and that 'the position of the United States is that the words "for construction, maintenance, operation, sanitation, and the protection of the said canal" were not intended as a limitation on the grant, but are a declaration of the inducement prompting the Republic of Panama to make the grant' of the Canal Zone to the United States in perpetuity.

"Though Secretary Hay mentioned the term, 'titular sovereignty of the Canal Zone,' he stated that such sovereignty is 'mediatized by its own acts, solemnly declared and publicly proclaimed by treaty stipulations, induced by a desire to make possible the completion of a great work which will confer inestimable benefit on the people of the isthmus and the nations of the world.' He also stated that it was difficult to conceive of a country contemplating the abandonment of such a 'high and honorable position, in order to engage in an endeavor to secure what at best is a barren scepter."'

"Later, on April 18, 1906, while testifying before the Senate Committee on Interoceanic Canals, Secretary of War Taft, when commenting in article III of the Hay-Bunau-Varilla Treaty, stated:

"'It is peculiar in not conferring sovereignty directly upon the United States, but in giving to the United States the powers which it would have if it were sovereign. This gives rise to the obvious implication that a mere titular sovereignty is reserved in the Panamanian Government. Now, I agree that to the Anglo-Saxon mind a titular sovereignty is * * * a barren ideality, but to the Spanish or Latin mind, poetic and sentimental, enjoying the intellectual refinements, and dwelling much on names and forms, it is by no means unimportant!

"Prior to that, on January 12, 1905, Secretary Taft, when commenting on the question of Canal Zone jurisdiction to President Theodore Roosevelt, stated:

"'The truth is that while we have all the attributes of sovereignty necessary in the construction, maintenance, and protection of the canal, the very form in which these attributes are conferred in the treaty seems to preserve the titular sovereignty over the Canal Zone in the Republic of Panama, and as we have conceded to us complete judicial and public power and control over the zone and the two ports at the end of the canal, I can see no reason for creating a resentment on the part of the people of the Isthmus by quarreling over that which is dear to them but which to us is of no real moment whatever.'

"This is not the last significant statement by Mr. Taft on this matter. On February 9, 1909, in an address delivered in New Orleans when he was President-elect, he said:

"'If the Hay-Herran Treaty of 1903 had been confirmed by the Colombian Senate, a failure to do which aroused our national indignation, we would not have been at all in the favorable position we are now to complete the canal.

"'Because under the treaty with Panama, we are entitled to exercise all the sovereignty and all of the rights of sovereignty that we would exercise if we were sovereign, and Panama excluded from exercising any rights to the contrary of those conceded to us. Now that may be a ticklish argument, but I do not care whether it is or not. We are there. We have the right to govern that strip, and we are going to govern it.'

"These forthright words of Mr. Taft, who was associated with the Panama Canal in responsible capacity longer than any other high U. S. official, should still the clamor of those who have been quoting him out of context.

"But Mr. Taft was not the last high official to speak out vigorously on Canal Zone sovereignty questions. On December 15, 1923, Secretary of State Hughes, in a conversation with Dr. Ricardo J. Alfaro, then Minister of Panama to the United States, declared with a refreshing degree of candor that the U. S. Government 'would never recede from the position which it had taken in the note of Secretary Hay in 1904.' To this he added: 'This Government could not and would not enter into any discussion affecting its full right to deal with the Canal Zone and to the entire exclusion of any sovereign rights or authority on the part of Panama.'

"Moreover, Secretary Hughes declared: 'It was an absolute futility for the Panamanian Government to expect any American administration, no matter what it was, any President or any Secretary of State, ever to surrender any part of these rights which the United States had acquired under the treaty of 1903.'

"In view of all the facts, the best case that can be made for Panama's claim of sovereignty over the Canal Zone is that of a reversionary character in the sole event of the United States ceasing to maintain and operate the canal. Should that ever occur, the United States would probably offer no objection to reassumption by Panama of sovereign control of the Canal Zone. Meanwhile, to encourage Panamanians to think that titular sovereignty is something that it is not, is lacking in forthrightness and counter to the best interests of the United States."

Congressman Flood's words summarize an exact position. If the concept of "titular sovereignty" is appealing to Panama's *dignidad* and *machismo,* by all means, in the interest of a Good Neighbor Policy, let us respect it. But above all, we must always delimit what it actually means, for to do otherwise would be unfair and hypocritical — a violation of the sound principles and best traditions of our national heritage.

If the youth of today rebels at any one factor in the societies of man, it can be said without equivocation that hypocrisy is the factor. "Credibility gaps" are merely the tearing away of veils of hypocrisy. In our relations with Panama we have the opportunity for candor. We have the opportunity to say what we mean and mean what we say.

The history and status of the United States position in the Panama Canal need not be obfuscated. The truth, without hypocrisy, is self-evident. Let us stand upon it and pass on to future generations of Americans this case in which our national interests are clear, in which our voice can be unwavering.

The issue of United States Panama Canal policy transcends domestic political differences. It lies outside of the pale of the cliches of "conservatism" and "liberalism." It requires nothing but the truth.

United States sovereignty in perpetuity over the Panama Canal Zone is unqualified so long as we live up to our obligations. If we do not intrude hypocrisy it shall rightfully remain ours. The opportunity to maintain our sovereignty over the Panama Canal Zone is not only an opportunity, but a national responsibility.

Chapter Three

The Intrusion of Hypocrisy

The United States of America, under Public Law 88-609, established the Atlantic-Pacific Interoceanic Canal Study Commission. This commission was assigned the task of studying the feasibility of a new so-called sea level canal for the Isthmus. To the extent of providing information on such a possibility it could have fulfilled a worthy purpose. To the extent of its speaking with a voice beyond its authorization it posed a perhaps well-intentioned, but still highly dangerous, element of confusion to our national interests.

A sea-level canal in Panama would require a new treaty. Without a new treaty the undertaking of such a project would entail flagrant violations of our 1903 Treaty with the Republic of Panama. These violations or the negotiation of a new treaty would imperil our sovereignty. This must not be permitted.

As we will show later, a new sea-level canal is economically and navigationally not only unnecessary and wasteful but as unsound an idea today as when it was first considered in the early years of the century.

What concerns us here is the incomplete, inaccurate and thus

15

misleading statements emanating from this commission, reflecting a tendency which can lead to the intrusion of hypocrisy into United States Panama Canal Policy.

Illustrative of this potential hypocrisy are statements made in a letter of February 24, 1969 to the Honorable Edward A. Garmatz, Chairman of the Committee on Merchant Marine and Fisheries of the U.S. House of Representatives, from the Honorable Robert B. Anderson, Chairman of the Atlantic-Pacific Interoceanic Canal Study Commission. Mr. Anderson is an influential Texas banker who has had a distinguished career as a public servant. Frank criticism of his statements in no way represents a slur on his character or his abilities. It is only presented in the spirit of bringing truth out into the open for the sole purpose of the preservation of the national interests of the United States which in other fields he has devoted much of his lifetime to protecting.

On April 16, 1969 Congressman Daniel J. Flood wrote to Congressman Garmatz a detailed analysis of certain statements contained in Chairman Anderson's aforementioned letter. The statements with Congressman Flood's comments are as follows:

"P. 1, par. 4, lines 6-10

"'The Commission has for some time held the view that a necessary step in the determination of feasibility (of a sea-level canal) would be an examination of the cost and effectiveness of meeting future requirements for transiting vessels from one ocean to the other by means of improvements to the existing lock canal.'

"*Comment*. Public Law 88-609 authorizing the current canal study has one and only one objective — a so-called sea level canal. The above quoted statement is a mere interpretation that does violence to the intent of the authorizing statute. In fact, a recommendation by the current study group for the high level lake and lock plan over a sea level plan would be contrary to the Act of Congress creating the commission.

"P. 2, par. , lines 1-5

"'H. R. 3792 would authorize construction of third locks at least 1200 feet long, 140 feet wide, and 45 feet deep. Such locks would not accommodate the modern angle-deck aircraft carriers of the U. S. Navy. Neither would they accommodate the ever increasing numbers of commercial ships drawing more than 45 feet.'

"*Comment.* The lock dimensions quoted are those of the Third Locks Project authorized by the Act of August 11, 1939 (53 Stat. 1409) on which project a total of $76,357,405 was expended, mostly on lock site excavations at Gatun and Miraflores. This expenditure, together with the estimated cost of $81,257,097 for enlarging Gaillard Cut, totals more than $157 millions toward the modernization program for the existing canal and is a substantial commitment by our government for it.

"The author of the letter does not show that the super commercial vessels now constructed, or that may be built, are designed for the purpose of avoiding transit of any canal for the reason that it is more economical to route them around Cape Horn or the Cape of Good Hope than to pay tolls. Nor does the letter disclose that the U. S. Navy long ago eliminated transit of the Panama Canal as a military characteristic in the design of large naval vessels and that the major ports of the United States are not designed to handle many of the super sized vessels, which require special facilities in deep water.

"P. 2, par. 1, last four lines

"'The completion of a third lane of locks would increase the capacity of (the) Panama Canal by about 50 percent. This additional capacity might be expected to care for traffic 10 to 15 years beyond the time the two lanes of the present canal become saturated *at the present growth.*'

"*Comments.* A recent report indicates that the maximum annual capacity of the existing Canal is about 26,000 vessels and that additional capacity will be required around 1985. During Fiscal Year 1968 the total number of transits was 15,511. The construction of a third set of locks will increase the capacity a minimum of 50 percent, bringing the total to more than 39,000 transits. Should this capacity be exceeded by traffic demands in the remote future something can be done about it at that time. Any other program than the major modernization of the existing canal is not realistic.

"Also to be noted in the excerpt just quoted is the author's apparent assumption that traffic will continue 'at the present rate of growth.' Such a premise makes his conclusions conjectural.

"P. 2, par. 2, lines 1-5

"'Elimination of the Pedro Miguel Locks would require that the existing Miraflores Locks be taken out of service for possibly four years while a third lift is added to the two lifts already existing at the site. This would require that all traffic pass through the single lane of new large Pacific locks.'

"*Comments*. Either the author of the subject letter has not read H. R. 3792 with sufficient care or he does not grasp one of its major features. This bill specifically calls for the 'consolidation of all Pacific locks near Miraflores in *new lock structures* to correspond with the locks capacity at Gatun.' The bill does not provide for the addition of a third lock lift to the existing Miraflores Locks as stated by Chairman Anderson but instead for their abandonment, with the elevation of the existing Miraflores Dam and its extension across the existing Miraflores Locks as shown in the diagrams on p. 133 of my volume on *Isthmian Canal Policy Questions* (Ho. Doc. No. 474, 89th Congress). This volume was distributed to all Members of the Congress and contains valuable data.

"The construction of the proposed new three lift locks south of Miraflores as contemplated in the pending bill would not in any way interfere with traffic in the existing canal. When the new construction is completed the new locks will immediately supersede the existing Pacific Locks (Pedro Miguel and Miraflores) without interruption of traffic. After the shift is made, the dam across Miraflores constructed, and the water level raised, the Pedro Miguel Locks can be removed and the needed Pacific summit lake anchorage supplied by necessary dredging.

"Furthermore, in regard to the statement in Chairman Anderson's letter about placing a third lock step on top of the existing Miraflores Locks, such procedure would place new concrete on top of old, which is opposed by many engineers. Moreover, it would require costly caisson construction work in Miraflores Lake which effort, in the opinion of independent engineers, could be made to far better advantage if devoted to the new locks. In fact, during the July 28-31, 1946, visit of Governor's Board of Consulting Engineers to the Panama Canal, this distinguished group opposed the location of new lock chambers on the existing Miraflores Locks. (See *Proceedings of the Consulting Engineers, Balboa Heights, C. Z., July 28-31, 1946,* p. D-27.)

"P. 2, par. 3

"'Construction of the third set of locks would leave unchanged the vulnerability of locks, dams, and power supply which makes the present canal extremely difficult to defend from sabotage or surprise attack.'

"*Comment.* Historically, the principal argument for a canal of so-called sea level design is that of relative vulnerability. In 1905-06, it was the threat of 'naval gunfire'; in 1939, it was the fear of possible 'enemy bombing attack'; in 1945-47, it was the 'atomic bomb and other new weapon dangers'; in 1964, it was sabotage with 'two sticks of dynamite'; and in 1969, it is defense against 'surprise attack,' as well as sabotage. No doubt we can expect new bugbears as new weapon systems are developed.

"Experienced independent engineers, nuclear and military authorities have repeatedly held that any type of canal is vulnerable to nuclear attack. The elimination of one set of locks would certainly simplify the problem of protection against both sabotage and surprise attack by reducing the number of vulnerable points requiring defense.

"As has been often stated by competent students of the canal question the true criteria for decision as to type of canal is not inherent resistance to enemy attack as may be embodied in design but ease and safety of navigation. This test leaves no doubt as to what the type of canal should be — one formed by lakes rather than a necessarily restricted channel at sea level. Furthermore, the plan contemplated in H. R. 3792, like that authorized in the cited Act of 1939, merely provides for an enlargement of existing facilities without calling for additional land or waters and does not require a new treaty with Panama. In contrast, a sea level project in the Canal Zone or a new canal elsewhere would require a new treaty with a huge indemnity and greatly increased annuity. Although such facts are paramount considerations that should be controlling and fully understood by all Members of the Congress, they have been, and still are being, ignored by advocates of a sea level project.

"P. 2, par. 4, lines 3-6

"'In addition, the third locks would require an increased operating staff, and require pumping of sea water for lockages. Both would increase operating costs by substantial amounts.'

"*Comment*. As to increased staff, experienced canal engineers have repeatedly expressed the view that the elimination of the locks at Pedro Miguel would simplify canal management and reduce operating costs at the Pacific end of the canal. These same engineers long ago studied the water supply problem and expressed the opinion that sea water for additional lockages can be pumped into the lake at a cost less than $250 per lockage, including interest, amortization and operating costs. (Ho. Doc. No. 139, 72nd Congress, p. 31.)

"In December 1968, I visited the Canal Zone and had an opportunity to engage in long discussions of interoceanic canal problems with various high officials and civilian leaders well informed on basic canal and defense questions. The views of these responsible individuals certainly controvert the main arguments set forth in the indicated letter. I summarized them in my statement to the House on 'Panama Canal Modernization: Time for Action Has Come' in the *Congressional Record* of February 19, 1969, p. H 1071."

From the *Congressional Record* of February 19, 1969 we quote this notable declaration by Congressman Flood:

PANAMA CANAL MODERNIZATION: TIME FOR ACTION HAS COME

On many previous occasions I have addressed this body concerning the vital subject of the Panama Canal. Although there is very little basic nature that has not been previously stated, the passage of time has sharpened our perspective and the assumption of office by a new administration makes necessary a reappraisal of the canal question in the light of the realistic considerations involved.

In this connection I would stress that, since the issues are fundamental, they transcend all partisan considerations and must be handled on the highest plane of statesmanship if our course is to be a wise one.

The principle questions in the interoceanic canal problem are:

First, the safeguarding of our indispensable sovereign rights, power, and authority over the Canal Zone for the efficient maintenance, operation, sanitation, protection, and military defense of the Panama Canal; also the security of the Western Hemisphere.

Second, the increase of capacity and operational improvement of the existing canal through the major modification of the authorized third locks project under what is known as the Terminal Lake-Third Locks solution.

Third, the matter of a second canal.

As to the first of the above three points, the Panama Canal is the strategic center of the Americas indispensable for hemispheric defense. Through an ill-advised policy of retreat at Panama and an unwarranted obsession with the glamorous old dream of a sea level canal, the executive branch of our Government has endangered our juridical status on the isthmus and proposed impossible treaty concessions to Panama. These, if adopted, would inevitably bring about chaos and disaster on the isthmus, with a total loss of our investment in the canal enterprise. This investment, including defense, from 1904 through June 30, 1968, was $6,368,009,000. Total recoveries during the same period were $1,359,931,421.66, which sum is only a small portion of the overall investment, making a net investment of over $5,000,000,000.

Fortunately, in 1967 the texts of the proposed giveaway treaties were published and some 150 Members of the House of Representatives introduced resolutions opposing their ratification. In this connection, Mr. Speaker, I would invite special attention of the Congress to the fact that the U.S. treaty negotiating team headed by Ambassador Robert B. Anderson ignored the provision of article IV, section 3, clause 2 of the U.S. Constitution which vests the power to dispose of territory and other property of the United States in the Congress and not in the Senate and executive alone. In either case, Ambassador Anderson and his diplomatic associates revealed their disregard of this vital provision of the Constitution or else sought to conceal it.

In regard to the second point about increasing canal transit capacity, a total of $76,357,405 was expended on the suspended third locks project, largely for huge lock site excavations at Gatun and Miraflores, which are usable in the modernization program espoused by other Members of Congress and myself. In addition, the enlargement of Gaillard Cut at an estimated cost of $81,257,097 is due for completion in 1971. These two projects together totaling more than $157 million represent substantial commitments by our Government for the major increase of capacity of the existing canal — too large an expenditure to be disregarded.

With respect to the third point, Public Law 88-609 authorized a study of the feasibility of constructing a new canal of so-called sea-level design. The reporting date for this study has been extended to December 1, 1970. As pointed out by Senator Strom Thurmond, a careful student of canal problems, in a statement to the U. S. Senate on March 6, 1968, the studies authorized by Public Law 88-609 are of sea level projects and that consideration under it of high-level lake and lock plan does violence to the authorizing statute. Moreover, extensive clarifications in the Congress as to the relative merits of the various canal proposals justify the abandonment of the idea of a sea-level canal and informed congressional opinion concerning the current inquiry is that it is a sheer waste of money.

In line with past practices of mine, after adjournment of the 90th Congress, I made a voyage to the West Coast of South America via the Panama Canal. On the way south, my ship stopped at Balboa, thus affording me an opportunity for discussions with Canal Zone residents and briefings by Panama Canal and military authorities. On the return voyage, Balboa Harbor was so crowded that my ship could not lay over at the Pacific end of the canal as desired but had to transit to the Atlantic. If there had been a summit-level terminal lake at the

Pacific end, as there should be, my ship could have laid over at Balboa. Because of the indicated anchorage lack in the Pacific sector of the canal, I would reemphasize as forcefully as possible the tremendous need for such additional anchorage in line with provisions of measures now before the Congress for effectuating the improved third locks project.

Mr. Speaker, those on the Isthmus with whom I discussed canal problems during my recent visit there are well informed. They presented views derived from long experience in the maintenance, operation and defense of our vital artery of commerce in an area of endemic revolution and endless political turmoil, which is especially vulnerable to communistic revolutionary subversion.

After return to Washington, I received a number of letters from the Isthmus expressing appreciation for my interest and suggesting that instead of my having been briefed by those there they should have been briefed by me. In fact, there was a mutual briefing. For the compliment involved, I am very grateful.

In this connection, I wish to invite attention of the Congress, expecially of new Members, to the volume of my addresses on "Isthmian Canal Policy Questions," published as House Document No. 474, 89th Congress. This volume, which is based upon careful research and experience over several years of recent canal history, contains a wealth of authentic information on significant aspects of the canal problem.

Returning to my recent visit in the Canal Zone, I would like to summarize informed opinion there as regards the current studies and as to what should be done by our Government as follows:

First, that there is no need for a second interoceanic canal.

Second, that construction of a sea level project in the Canal Zone should not be undertaken.

Third, that the well known Terminal Lake-Third Locks plan for the existing canal provides the wisest solution of the canal problem and is best for Panama as well as for the United States.

Fourth, that undiluted U. S. sovereignty and ownership over the Canal Zone territory and canal must be retained.

Fifth, that the proposed new treaties of the last national

administration providing for complete surrender to Panama of the present canal, as well as a like surrender of any future canal that would be built at tremendous cost to our taxpayers, should be summarily rejected and that authorization should be promptly enacted by the Congress for completion of the improved third locks project.

During the fiscal year 1968, the Panama Canal transited 15,511 vessels. Any waterway that handles such a volume of traffic is not obsolete but efficient. In fact, the canal is more efficient now than when it was opened to traffic in 1914, for efficiency and obsolescence are entirely opposite in character. The canal is, however, approaching saturation of capacity and the time has come for our Government to provide for the necessary increase of facilities as developed from years of operating experience.

To this end, appropriate bills have been introduced in the Congress and are now pending. These measures, if and when enacted, will obviate the necessity for any further study of "sea level" canals. Moreover, they will provide a simple, commonsense, historically based solution that does not require a new treaty with Panama, thus enabling continued undiluted U. S. sovereignty and control of the canal and its protective frame of the Canal Zone and the clearing up of the entire canal situation, all at the least cost to our taxpayers. When the improved third locks project is thus completed it will provide for the needs of world shipping for a great many years. The needs of the present and expanding economy of Panama will be met, Panama will retain its independence, the Canal Zone kept out of Soviet hands, and the security of the United States, the Western Hemisphere and the entire free world will be safeguarded.

These are paramount considerations that cannot be obscured by any amount of sophistry or self-serving propaganda on the part of fatuous thinkers and partisan advocates of the old idea of a so-called sea level canal.

*   *   *

Parts of these lengthy remarks by Congressman Flood are

highly technical, but they are important as supporting evidence of what must be said.

To the reader who may not have the time to grasp all of this data we want to emphasize that bills before the Congress provide for improvement of the Panama Canal within the existing framework of our treaty with Panama, i.e., they provide for, in Congressman Flood's words, the retention of "undiluted U.S. sovereignty and ownership over the Canal Zone territory and canal."

The danger of the acceptance of shaky positions such as those that can lead from Mr. Anderson's statements is that such positions can provide golden opportunities for the enemies of the United States to gain a wedge towards diminishing our sovereign rights in the Canal Zone.

This wedge can be gained by contradictions and unsound arguments which may intrude into our policy. These contradictions have not yet entered U. S. Panama Canal Policy, and we must not permit them to enter.

The Trojan horse for the admission of hypocrisy in our Panama Canal policy can easily be through contradictory technical jargon used by an uncareful technocracy. It is to this technocracy that Chairman Anderson has apparently and regrettably fallen victim.

The bills for major modernization of the present Canal were conceived by and are supported by those with the weight of experience in interoceanic canal problems.

Those who have supported the major modernization of the lake-lock type of canal as provided in the Thurmond-Flood bills include the following well-informed leaders: William B. Collier, Professor Donald M. Dozer, Captain Miles P. DuVal, Jr., Dr. Walter Darnell Jacobs, Major General Thomas A. Lane, Dr. Leonard B. Loeb, Dr. Howard A. Meyerhoff, William R. McCann, E. Sydney Randolph, William E. Russell, C. H. Schildhauer, Vice-Admiral T, G. W. Settle, John Kane, John F. Stevens, Jr., Professor Lewis A. Tambs and George M. Wells among others.

It is the considered judgment of these experienced gentlemen that major modernization provides all that is presently needed for improving the Panama Canal, both from engineering and navigational points of view, as well as for the full protection of United States sovereignty over the Canal Zone.

It would have behooved Chairman Anderson to personally study these proposals, although outside of the jurisdiction of his Commission, before having ventured to submit the most expensive ($25,000,000) book ever written, which played into the hands of those seeking to undermine the United States.

Every official of the United States should speak thoughtfully and with a clarion voice when discussing United States interests in the Panama Canal. To do otherwise, as Chairman Anderson did, permits the intrusion of hypocrisy into this vital issue.

Chapter Four

The Battle of the Levels

The permanent protection of United States sovereignty over the Panama Canal Zone was firmly ensured by the outcome of the "Battle of the Levels" in 1906. Senator Strom Thurmond, an astute student of canal problems, has said, "one of the basic decisions in the construction of the Panama Canal was the question of type decided after full debate in the Congress in 1906 in favor of the high-level lake and lock plan under which the Canal was built and has been subsequently operated."

The wisdom of that decision has been amply demonstrated by the passage of time. The primary credit for it is due to John F. Stevens, then Chief Engineer of the Isthmian Canal Commission. This remarkably able American won from his endeavors his greatly deserved fame as the basic architect of the Panama Canal. If any American is deserving of inclusion in our national Hall of Fame, John F. Stevens is so deserving.

In an article entitled "Isthmian Canal Policy — An Evaluation" prepared by Captain Miles P. DuVal, U.S. Navy (Retired) for the U.S. Naval Institute at the request of the Board of Control of the U.S. Naval Institute and published in the

March 1955 issue of the Institute's *Proceedings*, the "Battle of the Levels" is admirably sketched:

"Work under the United States control started haltingly, with increasing uncertainty as to the type of canal that should be constructed — the high-level lake and lock type or a canal at sea level. Each proposal had strong advocates.

"Fortunately, when the time for decision approached, President Theodore Roosevelt selected the great railroad builder, explorer, and business executive, the late John F. Stevens, as Chief Engineer of the Isthmian Canal Commission.

"Mr. Stevens' qualifications were unique. He had read everything available on the proposed Panama Canal since the time of Philip II, built railroads in the Rocky Mountains, and supervised open mining operations in Minnesota. Thus, in his experience he had witnessed what occurs when the balances of nature are altered, and understood the hazards involved in excavating a navigation channel through mountains.

"Arriving on the Isthmus on July 25, 1905, at the height of a crisis, he had matters under control within 24 hours. Experienced as he was in large undertakings, he promptly provided housing for employees, organized commissaries, encouraged sanitation, ordered equipment, planned the transportation system, and formed the basic engineering organization for building the Panama Canal. Indeed, so rapid was his progress that he found himself hampered by having to wait for a decision as to the type of canal, then being considered by an international Board of Consulting Engineers.

"In its report of January 10, 1906, this board split — eight members, including five Europeans, voting for "sea level"; and the five remaining Americans voting for high-level-lake and lock. The naval member on the Isthmian Canal Commission at that time was the Chief of the Bureau of Yards and Docks, who, in a minority report, favored the 'sea level' plan as 'affording greater immunity from hostile injury.'

"Meanwhile at Panama, Stevens had walked through the entire length of the canal route and studied the topography. Interpreting it in the light of navigational requirements as well as construction, he decided upon the high-level lake and lock plan, with the Atlantic terminal dam and locks at Gatun. For the Pacific end, he favored placing its locks in one group south of Miraflores at Aguadulce, just as he planned to do at Gatun.

"Testifying in Washington before congressional committees in January 1906, with a conviction for the high-level plan that no one could shake, he voiced his determined opposition to the 'sea-level' idea.

"But one appearance was not enough. In June, he was again in Washington, still leading in this memorable struggle, later described by Panama Canal historians as the 'battle of the levels.' On this occasion, Stevens even more forcefully and fearlessly urged the high-level-lake plan as the logical solution.

"In the end, with the support of President Theodore Roosevelt, Secretary of War William H. Taft, and the Isthmian Canal Commission, the recommendations of Chief Engineer Stevens prevailed. Congress, by the act approved June 29, 1906, adopted the high-level lake and lock plan as proposed by the minority of the International Board of Consulting Engineers. That was the great decision in building the Panama Canal, for the second time completing the pattern of interoceanic canal political and engineering debate.

"Here it should be noted that when making his recommendation to the Congress for this action, President Roosevelt did so after evaluating all available evidence of relative vulnerability and operational effectiveness of the two types. Although he understood that the 'sea-level' type would be 'slightly less exposed to damage in event of war,' he recommended the high-level plan because of its economic and operational superiority."

The intervening years have not lessened that economic and operational superiority. The ill-advised partisans of reviving the dead "sea-level canal" controversy have no new ammunition.

On the other hand, the achievements of science have brought about new question marks — unknown in Stevens' day — to plague a sea-level type canal proposal.

In the January 1969 issue of *BioScience*, magazine of the American Institute of Biological Sciences, is an article by

Professor John C. Briggs, Chairman of the Department of Zoology, University of South Florida. Excerpts from this important article follow to acquaint the reader with an aspect the sea-level canal advocates would like to ignore:

"While the possibility of a sea-level canal somewhere in the vicinity of the Isthmus of Panama has been discussed for many years, its feasibility as an engineering project has become enhanced as the result of recent experimental work with nuclear devices that can be used for excavation. It appears now that the undertaking of this project will be strongly supported as soon as the current economic crisis in the United States is over. Until recently, the only facet of the plan that had drawn the attention of many biologists was the possibility of radiation damage. However, Rubinoff (1968) finally pointed out that there would be other important biological effects and gave examples of disastrous invasions that have occurred in other places as the results of human interference.

"The New World Land Barrier, with the Isthmus of Panama forming its narrowest part, is a complete block to the movement of tropical marine species between the Western Atlantic and Eastern Pacific. . . .

"How effectively would a sea-level ship canal breach the New World Land Barrier? The engineering problems have been worked out using scale models. Although the mean sea-level is 0.77 feet higher on the Pacific side, it would have little effect compared to the effect of the difference in tidal amplitude. The tidal range on the Pacific side is often as great as 20 feet while it is usually less than a foot on the opposite side. For an open canal, it has been calculated that the tidal currents would attain a velocity of up to 4.5 knots and would change direction every 6 hours (Meyers and Schultz, 1949). Tide locks would probably be employed to regulate the currents and it seems apparent that the vast amount of fluctuation and mixing would provide ample opportunity for most of the marine animals (as adults or as young stages) to migrate in either direction. . . .

"A logical prediction can be made most easily if the pertinent information given above is summarized as follows:

1) The great majority of the species on either side of the Isthmus are distinct, at the species level, from those of the opposite side.

2) The habitats on each side of the Isthmus are probably ecologically saturated so that maximum species diversity has been achieved.

3) The Western Atlantic Region includes a much larger area, exhibits more habitat diversity, and possesses a richer fauna than the Eastern Pacific or Eastern Atlantic Regions.

4) Western Atlantic species are apparently competitively dominant to those of the Eastern Atlantic — a smaller region but comparable in size and habitat diversity to the Eastern Pacific.

5) At least some of the dominant species that have invaded the Mediterranean via the Suez Canal seem to be replacing the native species.

6) When the land bridge to South America was re-established, the invasion of North American mammals enriched the total fauna. However, this effect was temporary since so many native South American mammals became extinct that the number of species soon returned to about its original level.

7) A sea-level canal would provide ample opportunity for marine animals to migrate in either direction. This would probably result in the Eastern Pacific being invaded by over 6000 species and the Western Atlantic being invaded by over 4000 species.

"For the tropical Eastern Pacific, it is predicted that its fauna would be temporarily enriched but that the resulting competition would soon bring about a widespread extinction among the native species. The elimination of species would continue until the total number in the area returned to about its original level. *The fact that a large scale extinction would take place seems inescapable.* It would be difficult, and perhaps irrelevant, to attempt a close estimate of the number of Eastern Pacific species that would be lost. The irrevocable extinction of as few as 1000 species is about as appalling as the prospect of losing 5000 or more. . . .

"Man has undertaken major engineering projects for most of

his civilized history and the construction of such necessary facilities as canals, dams, and harbors will continue and expand as the human population grows larger. In this case, however, man would remove a major zoogeographic barrier that has stood for about three million years. The disturbance to the local environment would not be nearly as important as the migration into the Eastern Pacific of a multitude of species that would evidently be superior competitors. So, instead of having only local populations affected, the very existence of a large number of wide-ranging species is threatened. This poses a conservation problem of an entirely new order of magnitude.

"Rubinoff (1968) assumed that a sea-level canal would be constructed and looked upon its advent as an opportunity to conduct the greatest biological experiment in man's history. As I have stated elsewhere (Briggs, 1968), this approach is unfortunate for it tends to divert attention from a vital conservation issue. The important question is: Should the sea-level canal project be undertaken at all? What is the value of a unique species — of thousands of unique species? Currently, many countries are expending considerable effort and funds in order to save a relatively few endangered species. The public should be aware that international negotiations now being carried on from a purely economic viewpoint are likely to have such serious biological consequences. Does our generation have a responsibility to posterity in this matter?

"A biological catastrophe of this scope is bound to have international repercussions. The tropical waters of the Eastern Pacific extend from the Gulf of Guayaquil to the Gulf of California. Included are the coasts of Ecuador, Colombia, Panama, Costa Rica, Nicaragua, Honduras, El Salvador, Guatemala, and Mexico. While the prospect of such an enormous loss of unique species is something that the entire world should be aware of, these countries are the ones that will be directly affected since their shore faunas will probably be radically changed.

"Assuming that a better canal would provide economic benefits, I suggest either an improvement of the existing structure or the construction of a new overland canal that would still contain freshwater for most of its route. There seems to be no reason why we cannot have a canal that could accommodate ships of any size yet still maintain the freshwater barrier that is so important. One could conceive of other alternatives such as a sea-level canal provided with some means of killing the migrating animals — possibly by heating the water or adding lethal chemicals. However, such expedients would be both risky and distasteful. . .''

In the April 1969 issue of *BioScience* an interesting exchange of views took place between John P. Sheffey of the Atlantic-Pacific Interoceanic Canal Study Commission and Professor Briggs. Mr. Sheffey wrote:

"Professor John C. Briggs' article (*BioScience*, January 1969, pg. 44) points out some valid and important considerations in the coming decision on whether to build an isthmian sea-level canal. However, I hope you will bring to your readers' attention some factors that would tend to mitigate some of the alarms Briggs has cited.

"Our engineers calculate that there will be no net flow from the Atlantic to the Pacific through a sea-level canal. The approximately one foot higher mean sea-level of the Pacific will make the net flow from the Pacific to the Atlantic. Briggs' article indicates that biota carried in this direction pose the lesser threat in comparison with movements in the opposite direction. It appears that only the creatures that can swim against the current will be able to make the transit from the Atlantic to the Pacific.

"Briggs makes no mention of the transfer of marine life through the existing lock canal. In its 54 years of operation there have been and continue to be extensive transfers by three distinct means. First, swimming and drifting biota that thrive in both salt and fresh water readily pass through the locks and inevitably make their way across Gatun and Miraflores Lakes to the opposite oceans. Some have been specifically identified as having followed this path. Second, barnacles and similar clinging organisms pass in both directions every day on the hulls of ships. Third, and perhaps most important to the question of the biological impact of linking the oceans, is the daily transfer of fairly large amounts of salt water in ships' ballast tanks. This has gone on for more than a half century. Lightly loaded or empty ships approaching the canal are frequently required to take on ballast water before entering the locks. This is to deepen their drafts to make them easier to handle while in restricted canal channels. As a usual practice on leaving the canal a few hours later at the opposite ocean, this ballast water is discharged to lighten the ships to save fuel on the remainder of the trip. Thus, all the small swimming and drifting marine life that would be found in these thousands of samples of sea water taken year in and year out since 1914, have made the trip across the isthmus in salt water in both directions. While a sea-level, salt-water channel between the oceans would vastly augment the movements of marine creatures between the oceans, the new avenue would appear to offer previously denied passage for only that portion of ocean life that could not transit by one or more of the three existing means. Some segments of the total spectra of biota in the two oceans have surely crossed the isthmus to the opposite ocean during the past half century and continue to do so daily. It follows that a large portion of the small swimming, drifting, and clinging creatures on both sides of the isthmus have long been exposed to inoculations of the same category from the opposite ocean. To date, no discernible effects have resulted. It seems reasonable to conclude that a sea-level canal would create little or no new threat to the lower links of the ocean food chain. New exposures would be limited to the larger swimming and drifting biota. Thus the area of danger of harmful biological changes when the oceans are joined is much less broad than it first appears.

"Under a contract with the Canal Study Commission the Batelle Memorial Institute is conducting an extensive evaluation of the potential biological impacts of a sea-level canal. It is acknowledged that in the time available this study cannot reach final conclusions, but it can narrow the area of doubt. The Commission has arranged with the National Academy of Sciences to develop a program of bioenvironmental studies for the

Commission to recommend in its report to the President, should construction of a sea-level canal be recommended. Such a canal would require 12 to 15 years to construct, and hence ample time for biological research would be available.

John P. Sheffey
Atlantic-Pacific Interoceanic
Canal Study Commission
Washington, D.C.

Professor Briggs' reply is indicative of the type of forthright reasoning that is needed to illuminate the faulty reasoning of sea-level canal proponents:

"Since John P. Sheffey kindly sent me a copy of his February 6th letter to you, I have the opportunity to respond to his comments. If you decide to publish his letter, I would appreciate it if you would also consider the following:

"Mr. John P. Sheffey's main concern was that I made no mention of the transfer of marine life that takes place through the existing canal. Although many organisms have undoubtedly been transported by clinging to the hulls of ships or by living in the saltwater of ship's ballast tanks, the important point is that such transfers have not generally resulted in successful colonizations. For this reason, marine biologists have not been particularly interested in evaluating them.

"It would be a tragic error for us to conclude that, because the present canal has not served as a successful migratory route, there is no danger of a new sea-level canal doing so. How can there be any doubt that an open canal, providing a continuous salt-water passage between the oceans, would present a far better opportunity for successful migration? Many Red Sea animals have succeeded in passing through the Suez Canal to colonize the Mediterranean despite having to overcome formidable temperature and salinity barriers. Since a sea-level Panama canal would contain no such barriers, one can only expect that a huge number of successful migrations would take place.

"Considering that the mean sea-level of the Pacific side is 0.77 feet higher than the Atlantic, a very small net flow toward the Atlantic would take place. However, the gradient would be so slight — about 0.2 inches per mile — that it would have little effect compared to the difference in tidal amplitude. The tidal currents would cause so much fluctuation and mixing that it seems reasonable to conclude that most marine animals would have ample opportunity to migrate in either direction. We must also bear in mind that many planktonic as well as large organisms have sufficient swimming ability to counteract the effect of a slow net flow in one direction. Finally, we should recognize that many of the benthic invertebrate species will be able to colonize the sides and bottom of the canal itself and, by this method, could slowly extend their populations from one ocean to the other.

"I believe that the only dependable means by which large scale migrations and subsequent biological disaster in the tropical Eastern Pacific can be prevented is by the inclusion of an extensive freshwater barrier. The Atlantic-Pacific Interoceanic Canal Study Commission, with Mr. Sheffey as its Executive Director, has the responsibility of determining the feasibility of a new canal. It will make its final report to President Nixon in December, 1970. Biologists who wish to lend their support to the freshwater barrier concept should make their views known to the Commission and to their Congressmen.

John C. Briggs
University of South Florida, Tampa

But the bureaucratic, financial and political interests were to sweep all ecological considerations opposing a sea-level canal under the rug. How this happened is described in an article in the January 29, 1971 issue of *Science*, organ of the American Association for the Advancement of Science:

Sea-Level Canal: How the Academy's Voice Was Muted

Last fall a special presidential commission recommended that a sea-level canal be built across the Isthmus of Panama not far from the site of the present Panama Canal. The Canal Study Commission — officially known as the Atlantic-Pacific Inter-

oceanic Canal Study Commission — argued that the potential
military, economic, and foreign policy benefits justified spending
some $2.88 billion to build a sea-level passage that would
supplement and supersede the existing lock passage. The commission gave scant credence to assertions that a sea-level canal
might pose serious ecological hazards. Indeed, it devoted only 4
pages of its 109-page cover report to environmental considerations, and the thrust of its conclusions was that whatever
ecological risk might exist is "acceptable."

But this was not quite the view, it turns out, of a National
Academy of Sciences committee which studied the ecological
implications of the proposed canal at the request of the commission. Ernst Mayr, professor of zoology at Harvard University
and chairman of the Academy's Committee on Ecological
Research for the Interoceanic Canal†, told *Science* the canal
commission has "minimized" the potential dangers cited by his
group and has "talked about other things" rather than confront
the issues raised by the Academy group. "We said that great
danger would result from building a sea-level canal, though we
can't prove it," Mayr said. "But they turned it around and said
that, since we can't prove it, the danger is minimal."

The canal study—the latest in a series that have been
conducted since World War II—was authorized by Congress on
22 September 1964. The members of the commission were
subsequently appointed by then President Lyndon B. Johnson
and they were reappointed by President Richard Nixon when he
took office. The commission was headed by Robert B. Anderson,
former Secretary of the Treasury during the Eisenhower Admin-

---

†Other members of the committee included Maximo J. Cerame-Vivas, Univer-
sity of Puerto Rico; David Challinor, Smithsonian Institution; Daniel M.
Cohen, Bureau of Commercial Fisheries; Joseph H. Connell, University of
California, Santa Barbara; Ivan M. Goodbody, University of the West Indies,
Kingston; William A. Newman, Scripps Institution of Oceanography; C. Ladd
Prosser, University of Illinois; Howard L. Sanders, Woods Hole Oceanograph-
ic Institute; Edward O. Wilson, Harvard; and Donald E. Wohlschlag, Universi-
ty of Texas, Port Aransas. The staff officer was Gerald J. Bakus, University of
Southern California.

istration. Its other members included Robert G. Storey, former dean of the law school at Southern Methodist University, who served as vice-chairman; Milton S. Eisenhower, former president of Johns Hopkins University; Kenneth E. Fields, retired Army brigadier general and former general manager of the Atomic Energy Commission; and Raymond A. Hill, a San Francisco consulting engineer. The staff director was John P. Sheffey, a retired Army colonel with considerable experience in Panama. With the submission of its report on 30 November 1970, the commission went out of business.

Military and Economic Rationale

The commission's chief conclusions were that there are no insuperable technical obstacles to the construction and operation of a sea-level canal, and that such a canal would be highly desirable for a number of reasons. From a military standpoint, the commission concluded that a sea-level canal would be superior to the present lock canal because it would be less vulnerable to destruction and because it would be able to transit large aircraft carriers which can't fit through the existing locks. From an economic standpoint, the commission concluded that the present canal will reach its traffic capacity toward the end of this century, thus cramping U.S. and world trade, and that it will be unable to handle the increasing numbers of huge tankers and bulk carriers which are already beginning to appear on the world's oceans. The commission consequently urged that a sea-level canal be built along what is known as Route 10 in Panama, about 10 miles west of the existing canal, provided that suitable treaty arrangements can be worked out. The commission recommended that conventional excavation techniques be used because "neither the technical feasibility nor the international acceptability" of nuclear excavation have been established.

In assessing the ecological implications of a sea-level canal, the commission relied heavily on a report prepared by the Battelle Memorial Institute with some help from the Institute of Marine Sciences at the University of Miami. The commission said that certain forms of marine life have been passing through the existing canal for 50 years on the hulls of ships and in ballast water yet "no harmful results have been identified." The commission also noted that marine biologists have offered divergent predictions that a sea-level canal might cause anything "from disaster to possible beneficial results." In order to clear up the confusion, the commission said, it asked Battelle to conduct a study—admittedly limited in time and money— which involved a literature survey, mathematical modeling, and a study of marine species collected from the general canal area.

The Battelle report, which was prepared by William E. Martin, James A. Duke, Sanford G. Bloom, and John T. McGinnis of Battelle's Columbus, Ohio, laboratories, acknowledged that "present knowledge of the marine ecology of the Isthmian region is not sufficient to permit anyone to predict, with certainty, either the short-term or the long-term ecological consequences of sea-level canal construction." But the Battelle team went on to say that it had found "no firm evidence to support the prediction of massive migrations from one ocean to another followed by widespread competition and extinction of thousands of species" (a prediction that had been made by others but not by the Academy group). The Battelle group said that barriers could be arranged to block the migration of species from one ocean to another, and it argued that differences in environmental conditions on the two sides of the isthmus coupled with the prior occupancy of similar ecological niches by analogous species would constitute "significant deterrents" to the establishment of any species which might manage to get through the canal. In particular, the Battelle group found it "highly improbable that blue-water species like the sea snake and the crown-of-thorns starfish could get through the canal except under the most unusual circumstances." The Battelle group also said it had found "no evidence for predicting ecological changes that would be economically deleterious to commercial, sport or subsistence fisheries."

However, the Academy group seems to have been much less sanguine about the likely ecological impact of a new canal. The Academy report stresses that "available information is altogether insufficient to allow reliable predictions of particular events resulting from the excavation of a sea-level canal in Panama." But its report goes on to note that previous canal projects have sometimes led to "economic disaster" for certain fishing industries and have made it necessary to launch costly programs to repair the damage. Though it acknowledges that no predictions can be made with certainty, the Academy group warns that a sea-level Panamanian canal might produce major adverse consequences.

One previous instance in which a new canal caused great damage, according to the Academy group, involved the invasion of the Great Lakes by the sea lamprey, a predatory fishlike creature found in the North Atlantic. For thousands of years the sea lamprey was barred from the inner great lakes by Niagara Falls, but a system of manmade canals then allowed the lamprey to penetrate the inner lakes where it fed ravenously on valuable lake trout and other fish. In only 10 years the annual catch of lake trout in Lake Huron and Lake Michigan fell from 8.6 million pounds to 26,000 pounds. "This was an economic disaster for the fishing industry, one that has since been repaired only by years of research that finally led to an effective control of the invader through a costly management program," the Academy group said.

Another previous instance of major impact cited by the Academy group was the Suez Canal, where studies have shown that transmigration and colonization of marine plants and animals occur; that mobile, active organisms and fouling organisms are generally first to make the transit; that large-scale population changes occur; and that "significant economic impact sometimes results." Mayr, the head of the Academy group, told *Science* that a certain valuable species of sardine found in the eastern Mediterranean seems to have been "considerably affected" by competition from a less desirable species that invaded through the Suez Canal from the Red Sea. Mayr visited Israel last year to review work done on Suez Canal effects by a group of scientists at the University of Jerusalem. He said the Israelis reported that the "most remarkable thing" they had found was that it was nearly impossible to predict just what marine life would manage to get through the canal.

Points of Disagreement

In assessing the possible impact of a sea-level canal through Panama, the Academy group disagrees completely with some of the conclusions of the Canal Study Commission and of Battelle. Whereas Battelle found it "highly improbable" that the sea snake would get through the canal, the Academy group said the poisonous snake—a potential menace to predatory fish and to the tourist trade—"should have no real difficulty moving through a sea-level canal." The Academy report also concludes that the canal itself would provide "a nearly optimal habitat" for certain large Pacific sharks and that these sharks "could become rapidly established on the Atlantic coast of Central America, unless an effective barrier is employed." And whereas Battelle said it found no evidence that commercial or sport fisheries would be affected, the Academy report warned that some species, including certain shrimp, could be replaced by economically less valuable species. Mayr told *Science* it is "an indefensible statement" to say there will be no adverse effects on fisheries since no one really knows what will happen. The Academy group also warned that a sea-level canal might allow passage of parasites and pathogens from one ocean to another where they might cause serious destruction of organisms that lacked natural resistance to them.

Mayr's general impression of the canal commission's report is that it has made a number of "casual" and "misleading" statements, and that it has set up some straw men and then knocked them down while ignoring the most important fears expressed about a sea-level canal.

In order to lessen the potentially adverse impact of a new canal, the Academy report stressed that it is "essential" to install a barrier of warm fresh water in the canal to block the transit of as many species from the colder salt oceans as possible. But the canal commission was not persuaded that such a barrier is necessary. It simply said that if "future research" indicates the need for a biotic barrier (in addition to the tidal gates which will be installed to control currents), then "it would be possible to install a temperature or salinity barrier." However, the commission did not include plans for such a barrier in its designs indeed, it noted that the cost of a thermal barrier would be "high" and that the supply of fresh water available for a freshwater barrier is "limited." About the only point on which the commission and the Academy group seem firmly agreed is that an agency should be designated to support and coordinate research that could shed light on the potential environmental effects of a sea-level canal. Mayr professed himself "delighted" that the commission has recommended such a research effort.

Why were the Academy group's views largely ignored by the commission? Mayr and some other members of the Academy committee complain that the commission and its staff were more concerned about the economics of world shipping and about military defense than about possible ecological hazards—a charge which certainly seems to be true based on emphases given in the commission's report. But if the Academy group is right in asserting that the proposed canal could cause major damage, then the Academy itself must bear part of the responsibility for failing to make its voice heard.

Like all too many Academy committees, this one seems to have been given an overly restricted role. The canal commission report states that Battelle was asked to make "a study" of potential ecological effects whereas the Academy was merely asked "to recommend a program of long-term studies to be undertaken if the decision is made to build a sea-level canal." Mayr insists that his committee and the Battelle group did essentially the same thing, yet the fact that Battelle was the organization officially designated to do the "study" enabled the commission to emphasize Battelle's upbeat report while minimizing the Academy group's warnings.

The Academy study was further restricted in that it did not grapple with the question of whether a canal *should* be built, but only with the question of *how* it should be built. As the Academy report states in its preface: "Evaluation of the need for a canal and the wisdom of constructing it were explicitly excluded from the committee's task—deliberations were carried on under the assumption that a canal would be built." Asked why the Academy group had made that assumption, Mayr said the canal commission had, in effect, told the group: "Look here boys. That canal is going to be built no matter what you say." Consequently, Mayr said, "We decided the best thing to do was to make the canal as harmless as possible."

A further factor that limited the Academy group's effectiveness was its failure to speak out clearly. The Academy report does not use very forceful language in describing the potential hazards of a new canal. ("Scientists don't like to make loud statements—they like to understate things," Mayr says.) Moreover, the Academy group was unable to proclaim its apprehensions at the time the canal commission's cover report was made public last November. Neither Mayr nor the Academy itself would release copies of the Academy report until they had been officially published by the canal commission, and that did not happen until weeks later—long after public and press interest had dissipated.

*   *   *   *

No one can seriously contend that a group of scientists, who are by no means expert on the economic and military issues involved, should make final judgments as to whether a canal should be built. But the scientists are in a particularly good position to make judgments as to the ecological costs involved and to insist that these costs be considered before deciding whether to go ahead with a canal. As it now stands, the canal commission does not seem to have given much weight to the possible ecological costs, and its failure to do so must be blamed not only on the commission, but also on the Academy, which allowed itself to be mouse-trapped into a restricted role in which its voice was inevitably muted.

Science, it is said, is systematized knowledge obtained and verified through exact observation and correct thinking. Man should not make a sacred cow out of science, but neither should he ignore the painstakingly gained fruits of knowledge that the scientific method has gained us. The sea-level canal advocates are determined to proceed — hang the consequences to our environment.

When one goes outside for a "bit of fresh air" in any of our major urban centers and finds out that he has been gassed by the pollutants of thoughtlessness, he can readily experience the results to our ecology of the type of thinking epitomized by the Anderson Report.

To add insult to injury, the American taxpayer is expected to finance the destruction of his ecology.

When funds are needed desperately on the home front, why should we consider spending many billions of dollars on an unnecessary sea-level canal which would:

1. Imperil our sovereign rights in the Canal Zone
2. Be indefensible in time of war
3. Be an engineering horror
4. Be a navigational monstrosity
5. Be a drain on our financial resources
6. And now apparently, from the scientific viewpoint, a menace to the balance of nature!

The United States has demonstrated enough of an aptitude for becoming involved in gigantic and irresponsible wastefulness. The genius of John F. Stevens, basic architect of the Panama Canal, once saved us from such a fiasco. Let us heed the warning signs in advance and not resurrect the "Battle of the Levels." Only a fool will reopen a combat which has already been won, as proven by sixty years of experience.

Chapter Five

The Terminal Lake-Third Locks Plan

In 1914 the Panama Canal was opened to world shipping. An almost miraculous engineering feat had been accomplished. Thousands of miles had been clipped off of the journey around the South American continent. The Straits of Magellan and Cape Horn were no longer maritime passageways of the first rank.

Yet, this engineering feat, remarkable as it was, was not without fault. The engineer's views had prevailed in certain details over that of the navigator. Improvements were in order.

More than twenty years ago, Commander Arthur Stanley Riggs, a prominent archeologist, historian, lecturer and naval officer, described the canal's defects very clearly in the *Congressional Record* (January 5, 1949). His remarks are as true today as they were then:

"First of all, however, is the natural question: 'What's the matter with the Panama Canal?'

"It has the defects of its qualities. It was imagined by the French. When they could not finish it, we took hold and with improved machinery, more cash and unlimited skills, brought a greater canal to a successful conclusion. But the Canal was conceived by engineers, built by engineers. The men who have to get the ships through were never consulted. As a result there are defects of design which create hazards that endanger every vessel going through. After all, the object of any canal is to afford safe and speedy transit for vessels, since it is cheaper to send certain cargoes by water than by any other means. The principal problems that canal transit presents are accordingly operating problems. Their solution is so obvious that anything beyond that solution is merely creating an unwarrantable liability."

*   *   *

It seems to me that when sound planning is absent from aspects of an overall sound plan, the thing to do is to rectify the planning as it pertains to those defective aspects, not to scrap the fundamental plan in favor of a theoretical fantasy, which even theoretically, let alone practically, promises the makings of disaster.

But in the twenty year interval since Commander Riggs' statement nothing of consequence has been done to improve the canal. The skill of the Panama Canal pilots has prevented a tie up or massive accident. But is it fair for us to place the burden on this human element when a sound, economical, navigationally oriented plan exists, just awaiting the authorization of the Congress to be implemented?

This plan, well thought out and specifically designed to complement the engineer's abilities with the experience of the navigator, is called the Terminal Lake-Third Locks Plan.

Its origins lie in the days of World War II when canal capacity was taxed and initiative was permitted and taken by canal experts seeking a solution to the long-standing navigational problems connected with the Panama Canal. The study reached the White House and received the approval of the President. Improvement of the Panama Canal was given high postwar priority. Yet this priority was to be transformed into inertia through the medium of the atomic bomb. Visionaries who could not see the great future use of nuclear power for generators to light our cities or to power our fleet, nor foretell political problems accompanying then unforeseen nuclear test ban treaties, said to the world that A-bombs could dig a new "big ditch." Some of our leaders became mesmerized by the spector of the giant mushroom and work stopped on the improvements the canal needed.

The test of time has shown that nuclear excavation of a new Isthmian canal is an opium addict's pipe dream. Such a project lacks the most elementary criteria of an engineer, a navigator, a statesmen or those entrusted with the responsibility of protecting the United States from national economic bankruptcy.

A nuclear excavated sea level canal would be nothing but a gigantic put-together toy suitable for the modern age. No matter how you put it together, it would be wrong.

By contrast, the Terminal Lake-Third Locks Plan represents a harmonious interaction of engineer and navigator, those who are most concerned with such matters, along with an eye on costs. In addition, this plan enables the maximum utilization of all work so far accomplished in the existing canal and can be constructed with every assurance of success at far less cost than any other design so far considered. It would not dislocate the economy of Panama and thus avoid consequential indemnities which that country would undoubtedly demand to cover the costs of such dislocation. Moreover, it would serve by this continued presence of the United States on the Isthmus to guarantee Panama's independence.

The Terminal Lake-Third Locks Plan in reality represents a *completion* of the Panama Canal according to the principles laid out by the basic architect of the Panama Canal, John F. Stevens, Chief Engineer, Isthmian Canal Commission, 1905-07, and the first to hold the combined offices of Chairman and Chief Engineer of the Isthmian Canal Commission, 1907. Stevens' concepts were followed on the Atlantic side of the canal, but not on the Pacific end.

The greatest problem on the Pacific end is dramatically illustrated in the frontispiece of this book, a view of Miraflores Lake and the bottleneck Pedro Miguel locks, located squarely across the south end of Gaillard cut. This picture clearly shows the navigational horror of the approach to the Pedro Miguel locks and permits easy visualization of how the elimination of these locks and the raising of the level of Miraflores Lake to provide a safe anchorage, along with the consolidation of all Pacific locks south of Miraflores near Aguadulce just south of the present Miraflores locks, as specified in the Terminal Lake-Third Locks Plan, would greatly improve the efficiency and operational adequacy of the Panama Canal. This consolidation, with abandonment of the present Miraflores locks, would correspond to the consolidated locks on the Atlantic side at Gatun.

A diagrammatic side elevation of the Panama Canal, modified and adapted to the Terminal Lake-Third Locks Plan, is shown below:

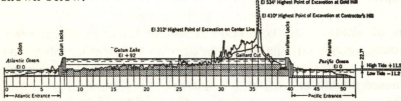

An excellent description of the Terminal Lake-Third Locks Plan is contained in the May 1957 *Marine Engineering Log* article, *"The 'Battle of the Levels' — Panama Canal"*:

"The Terminal Lake-Third Locks Plan covers several steps of improvement as follows:

"1. Removal of the bottleneck Pedro Miguel Locks.

"2. Construction of all Pacific Locks in continuous steps near Miraflores.

"3. & 4. Elevation of the intermediate Miraflores Lake water level (54 ft.) to that of Gatun Lake to serve as an anchorage during fog periods and to dampen surges.

"5. Raising the summit water level to its optimum height (approximately 92 ft.).

"6. Widening Culebra Cut.

"7. Construction of a set of larger locks."

Marine Engineering Log also summarized the advantages of the Terminal Lake-Third Locks Plan:

"1. Far less expensive than sea level plan. Part of the improvements started during the War on third locks could be used.

"2. No unknown geological problems.

"3. Terminal lakes at each end would provide for maneuvering or anchoring, meliorate the effects of fog, clear-cut operations on canal capacity and easier navigation.

"4. No diplomatic problems involved."

Point two, that of "no unknown geological problems," is only true of the Terminal Lake-Third Locks Plan. The sea level idea faces a separate set of geological conditions — a geologist's nightmare.

Dr. Howard A. Meyerhoff, Professor and Chairman Emeritus of the Department of Geology of the University of Pennsylvania, who is a specialist in engineering geology with personal experience in the field in Panama, says:

"A substantial — and formidable — part of the Zone, as well as of alternative interoceanic routes, consists of geologically young, poorly consolidated and unstable sedimentary rocks. At present canal elevations, slope instability resulting in slides has caused no end of trouble. An increase in the depth of certain of the cuts (Culebra, for example) by the difference between present elevation and sea level will increase the frequency and the volume of the slides during Panama's rainy season, roughly, by the square of the increase in depth. California's troubles during the torrential rains of last winter (and ante) illustrate the inability of sophisticated engineering to cope with the problem. Downward compaction of unstable material by nuclear blasts would actually aggravate the problem, as can readily be shown."

The weight of evidence mounts in favor of the Terminal Lake-Third Locks Plan. The truth inevitably will out, and the Sea Level Plan has been tried and found wanting.

Valuable time has been lost, but if it has served to settle the problem of our Isthmian canal interests once and for all it shall not have been in vain.

Now is the time to make the proper decision. Now is the time for procrastination to cease. Now is the time for each citizen of our country to stand behind Senator Thurmond and Congressman Flood and their distinguished colleagues, and be counted. It is our voice, that of an informed citizenry, which will be heard. And, God willing, ships will forever transit the Panama Canal in safety, under "Old Glory."

Chapter Six

The Voice of the People

The early June days of 1967 in our nation's capital forebode a long hot summer. The attention of the President was focused upon the mire of the Vietnam War. Like Br'er Rabbit's tar baby, the situation in Vietnam was sticky. LBJ had my sympathy in his troubles. He reminded me of the driver of a worn-out car on the Los Angeles Freeway at rush hour. He couldn't stay on, he couldn't get off. He couldn't accelerate, he couldn't decelerate. He couldn't face his real choice: to leave, or, preferably, to win.

To add to his worries the Middle East powder keg had exploded. In a classic, lightning military maneuver the Israeli armed forces immobilized numerically superior Arab forces and cut their way to the banks of the Suez Canal. When events were uncertain, the President was subjected to immense pressure from both sides of the conflict. Steadfastly he did what needed to be done — stay calm. He had my sympathy and admiration on his handling of this crisis.

A third issue L.B.J. faced was one in which I could not disagree with him more. He had initiated, certainly with good intentions, negotiations for three new canal treaties with Panama. But, like Topsy, they just grew out of hand. Ill-conceived and handled like a bull in a china shop, these proposed conventions amounted to a radical revision of our treaty arrangements with Panama. They would have compromised our sovereign rights over the Canal Zone. They opened the door for subversion of the Republic of Panama.

Latin American experts of varying philosophies recognized them for what they would be — a milestone of isolationism and a repudiation of the Monroe Doctrine, Franklin Roosevelt's "Good Neighbor Policy" and the American presence on which John F. Kennedy had sown the seeds for a hemispheric "Alliance for Progress." To conservatives and liberals alike — to all but the "old" and "new" isolationists — the treaties were "worse than a crime, they were a blunder."

Constitutionally, as they imperiled United States territory, the problem of treaty ratification lay not only within the Senate, but in the whole Congress — including the House of Representatives. It was there that the gauntlet was thrown down to the White House. It was there that the consensus of the people through their elected representatives was to be established. It was from there that this consensus was to spread. The proposed treaties *must not* be ratified.

I heard that Congressman Daniel J. Flood was to give a major address on this treaty. Sensing that this would be an historic occasion, I went to the Capitol to hear this speech.

Congressman Flood was no newcomer to Panama Canal matters. His father had been a friend of Theodore Roosevelt. As a boy the future Congressman had heard T.R. at firsthand tell the story of the history-making events leading to the construction and opening of the Panama Canal.

Those days in the early part of this century had previously been recounted to me by the late Commander Sergius M. Riis, a U.S. Naval Officer and Russian and Chinese expert whose uncle, Jacob Riis, had been a close friend of T.R. Through what Commander Riis had imparted to me, I could feel that those who had lived through the early days of the Panama Canal project had felt the same pride when the waters of the Atlantic and the

Pacific were joined that we felt in the summer of 1969 when our courageous astronauts first set foot on the moon. In both cases Americans had pioneered new dimensions and had conquered the unknown. In both cases our nation had become the steward of vast new responsibilities.

On the afternoon of June 7, 1967 the walls of our nation's capitol were to rebound with Congressman Flood's noble words. Sitting in the gallery I could visualize my counterparts of more than a hundred years past listening to the words of a Henry Clay, a Daniel Webster or a John C. Calhoun.

The Congressman began to speak. The mistake of the President in wavering from his previously firm position, and what that wavering had led to, were out in the open. But my thoughts were not on the President or those who lent their authority in support of a Presidential error. They were on such distinguished Americans as Vice Admiral T. G. W. Settle and Professor Donald M. Dozer who refused to accept a *fait accompli* and raised their authoritative voices in defense of our national rights, and Admiral Arleigh Burke who had the courage to publish their brilliant report.

But enough of comments on this historic address. The voice of the people was heard through the words of the "Conscience of the Congress" on the Panama Canal, Congressman Daniel J. Flood. Here are those historic words:

"PANAMA CANAL ISSUES AND TREATY TALKS": DEFECTS AND VALIDITIES

"Mr. Speaker, for the last decade, I have addressed this body many times on the subjects of the Panama Canal and interoceanic canals generally. As regards my attitude and judgments toward them, I assure you that I take no pleasure in registering disapproval of the administration, which, in general, I have supported. My views, however, are influenced by close associations going back to early youth and long study of the issues and problems involved. I cannot do otherwise than to speak as I do, for I must place my country above party in matters of such grave import as are now under discussion.

Furthermore, I believe that the President has been grossly mislead by his trusted advisers and that he has been beguiled into the adoption of policies that would be fatal to all concerned. I trust that he may become better advised and, in consequence, will take the position that many of us in the Congress who have studied interoceanic canal questions believe the wise and indispensable course for our Nation to puruse.

In approaching my subject, I wish to stress that the issues are fundamental. Thus, they transcend all personal or political considerations and must be considered on the highest plane of statesmanship. Also, I desire to emphasize that, as regards the Republic of Panama and its people, I hold both in the highest esteem, and have had the privilege of counting many Panamanians among my valued friends.

To the task of clarification, I now address myself.

Panamanian Mobs Attack Canal Zone, January 1964

Mr. Speaker, on the evening of January 9, 1964 at an American High School in Balboa, Canal Zone, on American territory, fine patriotic American high school students sang "The Star-Spangled Banner" and prevented Panamanian students from the Republic of Panama from lowering the U.S. flag and hoisting in its stead the Panamanian flag on the mast in front of the school. Seized upon by Red agitators and other radicals in Panama as a false motive concealing the real one, this incident was made the occasion for massive mob assaults on both ends of the Canal Zone that had long been planned as shown by their detailed preparations.

Overcoming the Canal Zone police, the invaders were well on their way to make the zone the scene of a Red bath of murder, pillage, rape, and sabotage, which was prevented only by the use of the U.S. Army stationed there for the protective purposes to defend the lives of our citizens and to prevent the damage or destruction of the Panama Canal itself.

This assault was a direct challenge to U.S. treaty-based rights, and power and authority over the territorial possession of the United States known as the Canal Zone.

Attacks on Canal Zone Focuses National Attention on Canal Problems

For 3 days, a reign of terror prevailed along the zone borders and in Panama. The volume of destruction of American property in both these areas was enormous and, so far as known, the total value of the property damage has never been calculated. Nor has the extent of the injuries suffered by our citizens in Panama ever been published or redressed.

Four of our soldiers were killed by Panamanian snipers and others wounded. Moreover, five of our citizens in Panama are reported as having been hanged and other atrocities committed.

Unfortunately, the mass news media of our country, following the Communist version, attempted to place responsibility for the instigation of the riots on our patriotic high school students, failed to report the cruel crimes committed against our citizens and property in Panama, and endeavored to create a sense of guilt on the part of the people of our country. Such failures and distortions of news, I attempted to counteract on March 9, 1964, in a major address in the Congress on the "Panama Canal: Focus of Power Politics"—House Document No. 474, 89th Congress, pages 305 to 344.

Mr. Speaker, at this point, I wish to emphasize that despite the gravity of the situation, the Panama Canal, lying in sight of the riot lines, continued to operate in normal manner, without interruption in transit. This notable achievement was possible only because of the loyalty and efficiency of our civilian employees of the canal enterprise and the effective work of the Canal Zone Police and our Armed Forces in protecting the lives of our citizens and the canal. Instead of having a sense of guilt as regards our successful operation of the Panama Canal, the people of our country, if they had known all the facts, would have taken great pride in the manner in which the 1964 Panamanian mob assaults were met and dissipated.

Regardless of the tragic consequences and the failure of the press to deal adequately with the attack on the Canal Zone, our citizens grasped the essential facts. Thus the situation at Panama made a greater impact on our country than any other crisis affecting interoceanic canals since the famous dash of the *Oregon* in 1898 from the Pacific around South America to join the fleet for the Battle of Santiago. Moreover, it started a chain of events affecting the canal that has not ended.

Panama Outmaneuvers The United States

Events occurred in quick succession. On January 10, 1964, the second day of the attack, Panama broke diplomatic relations with the United States, denounced the treaty under which the Panama Canal had been built, and subsequently maintained, operated, sanitated and protected, and filed a complaint with the Organization of American States charging "unmerciful acts of aggression" by the United States.

In a White House statement on January 14, immediately following the riots, President Johnson asserted:

The United States cannot allow the security of the Panama Canal to be imperiled. We have a recognized obligation to operate the canal efficiently and securely, and we intend to honor that obligation in the interest of all who depend on it. (*Evening Star*, Washington, D.C., Jan. 14, 1964, Stock Final edition, p. 1, col. 7.)

Notwithstanding this statement by the President of the United States, Panamanian officials kept up their agitations for renegotiation of the 1903 treaty, outmaneuvering our Government and placing it on the defensive. The result was that on April 3, Panama and the United States agreed to restore diplomatic relations and to appoint special ambassadors to consider the causes of the conflict between the two countries. Later, on December 18, 1964, President Johnson, reversing his forthright statement on January 14, agreed to negotiate a new treaty to replace the 1903 treaty and announced that our Government would proceed with studies for a new canal of sea-level design to replace the existing canal. These decisions, Mr. Speaker, were made on the advice of the President's ex parte advisers and without adequate inquiry or consideration. These advisers seem only to think of appeasement as supplying solutions.

Congress Authorizes Inquiry of a Predetermined Objective

Meanwhile, the Congress, on insistent administrative recommendations, enacted Public Law 83-009, approved September 22, 1964, for the "purpose of determining the feasibility of, and the most suitable site for, the construction of a sea-level canal" across the American Isthmus.

The legislative history of this statute is truly amazing. In the Senate, the bill was passed by voice vote without debate after perfunctory hearings, attended only by those supporting the pending legislation. In the House, I testified before the Committee on Merchant Marine and Fisheries on June 4, 1964, voicing strong opposition to the administration bill, which was narrow and limited in scope, and precluded the study of any other plan or the appointment of a broadly based and independent body to the required study. I urged the creation of a broadly constituted and independent Interoceanic Canals Commission.

The impact of my testimony was obvious, with evidence of approval on the part of certain members of the committee, indications of great interest on the part of representatives of the press who attended, and confusion and distress on the part of advocates of the pending legislation who were present. When news stories of the hearings were published in the mass news media the statements of the official witnesses were prominently featured and my own was completely ignored.

The hearings on this important measure, contrary to custom, were never published and the House was called upon to pass the bill on September 1, 1964 under a suspension of rules that did not afford ample opportunity for debate—a gag procedure. For more complete information on this legislative history, attention is invited to two of my addresses on the "Interoceanic Canal Problem: Inquiry or Cover Up?" on April 1 and July 29, 1965, particularly their documentation—House Document No. 474, 89th Congress pages 428 to 516.

The inquiry that was authorized was not that of an independent and broadly based agency created under congressional enactment, but by a part time consulting board of five men, appointed administratively and committed in advance to a predetermined solution. Certainly, this was not the way that the vital canal question should have been approached.

Thus, in addition to the crucial question of continued United States sovereignty over the Canal Zone, the Isthmian situation was further complicated by authorizing an inquiry wholly ex parte in character; and our chief negotiator was later appointed as chairman of the five-man, sea-level canal study group in addition to his diplomatic duty as head of the treaty negotiating team.

Basic Canal Issues Must Be Understood

The situation thus developed was not accidental but brought about by amateur canal builders, policymaking theorists, and others in our Government who ignore the lessons of experience.

Because of the necessity for a clear understanding of the basic canal issues in connection with what will be later developed in this address, I shall repeat them:

First, the transcendent responsibility of our Government to safeguard our indispensable sovereign rights, power, and authority over the Canal Zone for the efficient and adequate maintenance, operation, sanitation, and protection of the Panama Canal.

Second, the subject of the major increase of capacity and operational improvement of the existing canal through the modification of the authorized third locks project—53 Stat. 1409—to provide a summit-level lake anchorage in the Pacific sector of the Panama Canal to correspond with the layout in the Atlantic end, on which project some $75,000,000 was expended, largely on enormous lock site excavations at Gatun and Miraflores before work was suspended in May 1942; and which excavations could contribute materially toward the suggested lake-lock type of improvement for the present canal.

Third, the question of a new Panama Canal of so-called sea-level design, or modification thereof, to replace the existing canal.

Fourth, the matter of the construction and ownership of a second canal at a site other than the Canal Zone, including Nicaragua, and treaties therefor.

From the above it is obvious that the principal canal policy questions, as historically evolved, are the best type at the best site for vessels of commerce and war of all nations on terms of equality as provided by treaty and at low cost of construction, maintenance, operation, sanitation and protection. Have our amateur canal builders and policymakers attempted to clarify these issues in realistic manner? They have not, but have tried to cover their operations with the mantle of secrecy and confusion. Nevertheless, in view of what I shall later state in this address, these key issues must be thoroughly understood and brought into the open.—See House Document No. 474, 89th Congress, pages 177 to 192.

Panamanian Blackmailing Propaganda Against The United States

The story of the successful effort of the United States in the acquisition of our Canal Zone territory and its sanitation, the construction of the Panama Canal, and its subsequent maintenance, operation, and defense, constitutes one of the most outstanding and inspiring chapters of American history. Yet, the communistic treatment of all this has been seized upon and exploited by Panamanian radicals to the effect that the United States has been guilty of the grossest selfishness and imperialistic and oppressive design. There could be no greater falsehood.

Constantly repeated in the press of the United States, this adverse propaganda has not only had the effect of creating a wide spread sense of shame among certain bleeding heart "liberals" and "intellectuals" of our country but also to brainwash and cow our negotiators and the President of the United States himself.

No one in the executive branch of our Government since early 1964 has ventured any statement of contradiction and this harmful propaganda of self-condemnation has been allowed to circulate without rebuttal, creating a condition conducive to political blackmail.

Thus, Mr. Speaker, a most glorious chapter of our history has been, and is still being, distorted into an infamous chronicle. In the atmosphere so created, new treaties with Panama have been proposed for the surrender of our indispensable rights and authority with respect to both the Panama Canal and Canal Zone.

As to such nefarious cession, I quote the 1923 statement of Secretary of State Charles Evans Hughes, who, when faced with a similar situation, called in the Minister of Panama and bluntly stated to him:

It was an absolute mutility for the Panamanian Government to expect any American administration, no matter what it was, any President or any Secretary of State, ever to surrender any part of these rights which the United States had acquired under the treaty of 1903. (*Foreign Relations,* 1923, Vol. III, p. 634.).

Why is it, Mr. Speaker, that no one in authority in our Government speaks that way today? There can be no adequate explanation except a news blackout induced by appeasers engaged in a conspiracy of silence and their exploitation of a sense of guilt created by false propaganda, originally initiated by Soviet authority.

Congress Tries To Counter The News Blackout

Recognizing the dangers involved in the failure of the mass news media to alert the people of our country, informed leaders of the Congress in 1966 brought about the publication of a volume of my principal addresses under the title of "Isthmian Canal Policy Questions"—House Document No. 474, 89th Congress.

This volume contains a wealth of carefully researched material on key canal problems and it was widely distributed throughout the Nation and to all Members of Congress.

With the information therein developed readily available, it should not be possible for the executive branch of our Government to stampede the Senate into ratifying the current treaty proposals with Panama by a surprise submission of the treaty or treaties with plausible pleas of emergency. Any attempt to do so on the basis of threats of possible renewal of Panamanian riots would, in essence, be a form of guerrilla warfare, which has no place in the Halls of the Congress.

Mr. Speaker, at this point, I would urge all editors, reporters and other publicists of the mass news media to study the indicated volume, which is available in Government depositories throughout the Nation or can be obtained without charge from Senators and Representatives. If the disseminators of news will present essential facts in the canal situation to the people of our country, the latter will know how to prevent the projected surrender and betrayal at Panama. The total book value of our investment in the Canal Zone from 1904 to 1966 provided by the taxpayers of the United States, as recently furnished by the Secretary of the Army, is $4,889,051,000. This is a startlingly large figure even in this land of prodigal spending—see Reports of the Secretary of the Army, April 10 and 21, 1967, quoted by me in a statement to the House of Representatives on May 10, 1967.

U.S. Policies Must Be Wise and Realistic

The U.S. diplomatic team for the current negotiations with Panama is purely an administrative body committed in advance to giveaway policies, and as already stated, with the Chairman of the Sea Level Commission created under Public Law 88-609 serving as Chairman of the treaty negotiating team. It is significant also that this body has no member experienced in military and naval features of the canal problem. This shows how narrow and provincial it is. It amounts to nothing more than a number of "yes men" named to do a specific task—giving away the Panama Canal with the mistaken idea that appeasement will settle all the problems involved. Certainly, this is not character- istic of statesmanship or vision of what the future may bring forth. Indeed, the whole diplomatic effort seems to have been, and still to be, to abase our nation and its wise and beneficent policies which have obtained for more than half a century with respect to the canal and to accept as true all that in recent years has been described as evil and oppressive on the part of the United States—charges emanating from communistic and demagogic sources. Such policy will in no wise close the lid of the box of Pandora but will open it wider and tremendously augment the confusion and chaos which our recent policies have already produced.

In truth and in fact those undertaking to act for the United States in the current negotiations with Panama are, in effect, acting not for the United States but for Panama and are motivated by the desire to do anything, however unwise or fatal, for the purposes of appeasement. The base surrenders in the projected new treaty proposals are justified by our officials to prevent riots of Panamanian mobs and assaults on the Canal Zone. Such a policy is unwise, unpatriotic, and oblivious of the requirements for the successful maintenance, operation, sanitation, and protection of the Panama Canal, thus imperiling the best interests of both the United States and Panama, and the world at large. The occasion demands a firm and just policy, and the present policy is neither just nor wise but is, in the opinion of many informed persons, altogether pusillanimous and contemptible. Like giving into blackmail such surrenders can only result in greater extorsions and our complete abandonment of the canal enterprise, with its takeover by Communist power, direct or indirect, and the destruction of Panamanian independence. Thus, Panama could become another Cuba. The radical policy now being pursued by Panama is absolutely suicidal.

Proposed Surrender At Panama Treasonous

The United States joined in World War I and II to defeat aggression against free nations and was largely responsible for winning those wars in the name of freedom. As so often is the case, what was won on the battlefield was lost at the council table. Then we went half way around the world to fight the Korean war to check communistic aggression. That war, an inglorious defeat for the United States, has never been ended but is in a state of "suspended animation." Now, also half a world away, we are fighting the war in Vietnam under the most difficult conditions and at tremendous cost and sacrifice to check communist aggression, and it is yet undecided.

Were it not for the support of North Vietnam by Red China and the Soviets, particularly the latter, our efforts in that area would have been crowned with success long ago with relief of South Vietnam and Southeast Asia from Red power. Because of the efforts of the two large Communist countries to infiltrate every nation in the Western Hemisphere from Cuba as a base of operations, we are kept on the brink of another war—in the Western Hemisphere—to stay the onward march of Red power.

In the light of all these facts is it wise or safe to divest ourselves of our just and equitable rights with respect to the Panama Canal, the maintenance, operation and protection of which must always remain with the United States if the cause of freedom is to be served? Is it not the sheerest folly and criminal stupidity at this critical juncture in world affairs to ignore the situation involved and render ourselves impotent through the surrender of the greatest factor in Western Hemisphere security?

We are indeed in actual war with the Soviet and Red China because both of these countries are accessories to the struggle now being waged in South Vietnam, supplying modern weapons, munitions, and training that are necessary for Red forces therein engaged. In view of these circumstances is not the attempt to dilute and destroy our treaty based and indispensable authority and control of the Panama Canal and its protecting Canal Zone frame, in essential fact, treasonous in character?

It is significant, indeed, as previously indicated, that on our treaty negotiating team there is not a single member with responsible military or naval experience. The only apparent reason for not including such really qualified members is that such men could never be brought to disregard the hemispheric protective factors involved and might be able to thwart the contemplated surrender.

*   *   *   *

Booklet On Panama Canal Issues and Treaty Talks Described

In the course of the last 2 years much adverse propaganda has been published about the canal situation, altogether lacking in objectivity and comprehensiveness. The latest contribution of significance is a booklet on "Panama Canal Issues and Treaty Talks" prepared by an unofficial nine-member panel of the Center for Strategic Studies, Georgetown University, which I have read with much interest and studied with care.

To a large extent, its statements of fact are based upon the information developed in my own researches and embodied in my addresses as published in the volume on "Isthmian Canal Policy Questions"—House Document No. 474, 89th Congress. Because publications by the Center for Strategic Studies are influential in molding public opinion and its Panama Canal booklet has serious shortcomings, I shall undertake to appraise it objectively.

The booklet consists of a "Preface" under the signature of Adm. Arleigh Burke, Director of the Center for Strategic Studies, a list of "Members of the Panel," a statement of the "Conclusions of the Panel," a "Majority Report" in part I, a "Minority Report" in part II, and "Appendix," consisting of a description of the "Choco Development Project" in Colombia and "Additional Notes About Panama."

It is evident from reading the booklet that there was much discussion and probably contention in the course of the proceedings of the Panel. It is significant that in the conclusions of the "Majority Report" there is this statement:

The members of the Panel have not directed their attention toward the merit of this (surrender) policy change, but rather, because it was a Presidential announcement, believe that the position (of surrender at Panama) is now established as a *fait accompli*.

The Majority Report's conclusions are premised on this erroneous assumption.

In contrast, the "Minority Report," prepared by Dr. Donald M. Dozer, a distinguished and experienced historian, and Vice Adm. T. G. W. Settle, an outstanding naval officer of vast experience, does not accept a Presidential pronouncement of intended action as accomplished fact but approaches the problem on the basis of the merits of the issues.

Preface Analyzed

The most significant part of the preface is that in which it lists
what are described as "key Isthmian Canal questions."

The first one on sovereignty, though it does not so state,
implies support for the surrender policy. As regards this, I would
say that, if and when the 1903 Treaty is annuled and the current
extreme demands of Panama are crystallized by a new treaty for
a short period then we may expect that Panama will in all
likelihood undertake to expropriate the existing canal under the
contention that the Canal Zone has passed back wholly and
exclusively to Panamanian jurisdiction, and that such right of
expropriation could be exercised by Panama within the purview
of international law.

Elsewhere, the "Preface" emphasizes that the "progress of
negotiations" has been "so limited" that it expresses the desire to
"help resolve the unsettled questions." In other words, the
"Preface" aims to expedite the surrender processes. This is an
open invitation to the people of the United States to support the
policy of surrender and betrayal at Panama, regardless of the
basic wrongs involved.

In order that the full text of the "Preface" may be easily
available, I shall quote it among the documents appended to my
remarks. I would urge all who seek to understand key canal
issues to compare this prefatory note with the basic canal issues
as summarized by me earlier in this address.

Conclusions of the Panel Majority Evaluated

The majority of the Panel as earlier stated frankly admits
that it supports the position of surrender at Panama as an
accomplished fact. As to such assumption, I would declare that,
under our Constitution, there could be no greater fallacy. The
majority conclusions unequivocally accept the viewpoints of the
present treaty negotiating teams and of the current canal study
group under Public Law 88-609. Their conclusions certainly do
not reflect the opinions and judgments of a host of informed
citizens of the United States, who include experienced statesmen,

officers of our Armed Forces, engineers, navigators, nuclear warfare and other experts of eminence.

Communistic influences in Panama will never permit a settlement of radical demands except by the complete withdrawal of all United States authority with respect to any Isthmian Canal. If mobs are permitted to dictate to the Panama Government then every surrender will lead to new mobs to bring about further surrenders and this process will continue until we are driven from the isthmus. It is the sheerest folly to believe that anything less than our complete abandonment of the canal enterprise will satisfy the communistic demands of Panama.

Mr. Speaker, if we cannot control the Panama Canal and Canal Zone over which we hold sovereignty in perpetuity under treaty grant with responsible treaty rights and which we own by purchase from individual owners, how can we hold any canal over which we do not have such authority and ownership and what is to prevent our country from being driven altogether from the isthmus? Then, who would control this vital interoceanic link and who would operate it to serve the needs of world commerce as required by other treaties to which we are committed?

Again, Mr. Speaker, I ask why should there be any change in the existing treaty as long as we have the existing canal? To say the least, any basic change as regards the canal and zone should be deferred until any new canal is undertaken and completed. Yet, in their maddened zeal to take over the canal, Panamanians demand immediate surrender of all our basic and indispensable rights over the canal and complete cession of the Canal Zone to Panama.

In view of the world situation with war clouds all around the horizon, including Latin America, the principal conclusions in the "Majority Report" are not only stupid but amount to criminal folly, and are in utter disregard of the taxpayers of the United States, the vast expenditures defrayed by our Government, the sacrifices made by the builders of the canal, and the security of the Western Hemisphere. The Congress ought to investigate this entire matter on its objective merits and advise the Nation at large of the identity of the miners and sappers in our Government responsible for the projected betrayal at Panama. They have grossly misinformed and misled the President.

Majority Report Support Panamanian Views

The greater part of the booklet under discussion is the "majority report," pages 3 to 67. It consists of a condensed historical summary from 1848 to June 17, 1966, a chapter on "The Dimensions of the Negotiation," another on "The Canal Studies," another on "The Special Problems of Nuclear Excavation," and, finally, one on "The Climate of Public Opinion."

Because my comments on various statements in the "majority report" are extensive, I shall not discuss individual points here except to state that virtually the entire "majority report" is devoted to the support of the projected surrender and toward securing authorization of a vast construction undertaking in Panama that is wholly unprecedented in the isthmian area and unjustified from every practical angle.

Entirely unrealistic, the "majority report" fails to evince the fact that the grave concessions which have been proposed would not, if granted, satisfy extreme Panamanian demands but would be accepted by Panama as the justifying foundation for divesting the United States of its last vestige of control as regards the canal enterprise and for its complete takeover by the Panamanian Government. In this connection, Mr. Speaker, I venture the further prediction that if the United States is driven from the isthmus that Panama itself will lose control of the canal immediately because of Soviet domination.

As indicative of the short sightness of advocates of a new canal in the Canal Zone or in the Panama of so-called sea-level design is the fact that these partisans also urge a treaty of short duration under which the canal should be built and operated. Thus, after the U.S. taxpayers provide the vast sums required for its construction, indemnities and annuities, such treaty for a new canal will end after a brief period, and Panama will be privileged not to renew it with the result that our further investment will be wholly lost. If the people or our country understood what is thus involved they would voice justifiable indignation and resentment.

It is for reasons of this character that those responsible for the new treaty proposals are moving heaven and earth to keep facts in the present situation from becoming generally known. Thus, our taxpayers stand not only to lose the nearly $5 billion invested in the present canal and its defense but also the investment in the proposed new canal running into billions.

If such treaty proposals as those accepted by the "majority report" as accomplished facts, are ever ratified by the Senate, it will be because responsible administrative officials, in their fatuous pursuit of policies of appeasement and the practice of the un-American policy of managed news, were able to prevail. But when our people realize what has happened they will understand that the best interests of their country have been betrayed and their elected representatives in the Congress, influenced by such sentiment, will deal most charily with the subject of implementing appropriations. The present treaty negotiators of the United States, as reflected in the "majority report," show an absolute indifference to the best interests of our taxpayers and consider the interests of the Nation altogether inconsequential.

Moreover, it must be understood that in all the Central American states where a new Isthmian Canal might be constructed, Communist revolutionary influence is so strong and political instability so prevalent that a canal operated under any authority except the exclusive authority of the United States would not be an asset to our country but a detriment.

Panama Canal Cannot Serve Two Masters

Even now, under our extreme "liberal" policy with respect to the canal we are permitting the transit of vessels that carry munitions and other supplies for North Vietnam Armies. Thus, the canal is being made into an accessory in behalf of Red forces at war with the United States. This is bad enough as it is but it would be far worse if Panama is made a comanager of the canal.

In such event, Panamanian policy would be adamant against any use of the canal that might offend Communist powers and the result would be that our Government would be involved in a constant state of friction with Panama concerning matters of this character, and others less serious. Should the Panama Canal ever become a political plum for Panama it would be the target in ceaseless struggles between Panamanian factions for highly paid positions, with grave consequences affecting canal security. For efficient operations, the United States must have exclusive responsibility: and from this fact we cannot escape for the canal cannot serve under two masters.

It follows, therefore, that the United States must have, as it has always had, adequate authority to perform the tremendous tasks imposed by solemn treaty obligations and which, for more than 60 years, it has so wisely and efficiently exercised. The Panama flag now displayed in the Canal Zone equal with the flag of the United States with funds from our taxpayers is a symbol of divided authority and must be hauled down.

Minority Report Protects U.S. Interests

Though less extensive than the "Majority Report," the "Minority Report" repudiates the idea that a Presidential pronouncement is a "fait accompli" and evaluates the canal problem on the basis of merit. Drawing upon authentic independent sources of information, the authors reveal themselves as possessing a remarkable store of digested knowledge, with a clear and realistic understanding of the problems involved, and the capacity and courage to state their views with effective clarity.

Of particular interest to informed Members of the Congress will be the fact that the "Minority Report" contains a program for action by the United States. Because of its importance, I shall summarize its highlights:

First, Terminate immediately the present negotiations with Panama while holding Panama to strict and just accountability for respecting and enforcing its treaty obligations for the maintenance of law and order in the terminal cities of Panama and Colon.

Second. Withdraw any and all arrangements for shared management of the canal.

Third. Reassert the position of the United States in the sovereign control of the Canal Zone and Panama Canal.

Fourth. Insist upon Panamanian recognition of the full force and validity of the 1903 Treaty, allowing, however, an adjustment of the annuity in that treaty.

Fifth. Require, as a necessary condition to the resumption of treaty negotiations, that Panama agree to a revocation of certain major concessions made to her in the 1936 and 1955 treaties, which, in perspective, appear to have been only stepping stones for the ultimate takeover of the canal from the United States.

Sixth. Insist upon receiving from Panama in perpetuity the entire watershed of the Chagres River, necessary for canal purposes.

Seventh. Abandon plans for the excavation of a new canal of so-called sea-level design, whether by nuclear or conventional methods.

Eighth. Proceed with the improvement of the existing canal in accordance with the Terminal Lake-third locks plan in order to provide necessary additional transit capacity and operational improvement.

This program, Mr. Speaker, enables the maximum utilization of all work done to improve the canal since 1914, including that on the suspended third locks project. It is authorized under existing treaty and does not require the negotiation of a new one. Such improvement would provide a two-way ship channel in the summit level with ample lock capacity at each end arranged to provide optimum conditions for the convenient and economic transit of vessels. This is what the shipping using the canal needs and it is what they should have with the least possible delay.

United States Must Not Surrender Canal Zone Sovereignty

Mr. Speaker, when the Congress approaches the canal problem let us not be deceived by pleas of emergency in Panama, however plausibly expressed. Such entreaties are induced by timidity on the part of our officials who desire to create a fine "image" in foreign lands or by fear of Panamanian mob assaults on the Canal Zone. The President of the United States cannot know everything and has to depend on his advisers.

Is it not the duty of the Congress to protect him and the

Nation from irretrievable error inherent in a policy of reacting to contrived situations?

The struggle in which our contry is now engaged against aggressive communism is global and transcends all questions of partisan nature. The Panama Canal, as the key strategic point in the Western Hemisphere and the greatest single symbol of U.S. prestige and power, is marked for a takeover by Red revolutionary force. Its loss will serve as a mighty spark to encourage and activate Communist revolutionary overthrows of constitutional governments not only in other Latin American countries. Moreover, such loss would make a calamitous impact on other crucial strategic spots—Southeast Asia, where our fighting men are dying; Gibraltar, the gateway to the Mediterranean; the Suez Canal—already under Soviet domination—and the Red Sea, the transportation artery to the Indian Ocean; and southern Africa, which dominates the sea lanes around the Cape of Good Hope.

As important as our winning the Vietnam war may be in fighting Communist revolutionary aggression, the loss of that war would be less disastrous in its long-range consequences to the United States and the Western Hemisphere than the proposed surrender of the Canal Zone now being advocated by elements in our Government.

If the jurisdiction over the Canal Zone is ceded back to Panama it will mean that all the courts, schools, police and fire forces, and other civil activities will pass to Panamanian control. It will mean that all the public and private buildings in the zone erected and maintained at great expense by our Nation, including hospitals, barracks, military installations, school buildings, streets, bridges, and the like now bearing names bestowed by the Congress, directly or indirectly, in appreciation of services rendered by the builders of the canal, will become subject to a new system of nomenclature by Panama that will completely ignore the commemoration intended by our Government. Also, it will mean that the slums and brothels of Panama City and Colon will be extended into the Canal Zone area, bringing worldwide condemnation on the United States.

The Canal Zone is to our people a holy and sacred spot made

sacred by the services and sacrifices of those who built the canal
and have since maintained and defended it. Any policy or action,
by our Government to ignore these facts will constitute an
inglorious and abject effacement for what is dear and precious to
our citizens, and wake angry repercussions.

In view of all these facts, Mr. Speaker, under no circum-
stances should the United States cede its sovereignty over the
Canal Zone to Panama, for we would do so at the peril of
Western civilization.

Summation

In the way of summation of the principal points in the canal
situation, I would emphasize the following:

First. The United States has a fine canal at Panama now with
indispensable sovereignty and jurisdiction over the Canal Zone
territory for its efficient maintenance, operation, sanitation, and
protection but it is rapidly approaching capacity saturation and
requires operational improvement.

Second. Experience has shown that the present canal will
work and how to provide for its major increase of capacity and
operational improvement, without a new treaty with Panama.

Third. This modernization program, developed during World
War II and known as the Terminal Lake-Third Locks plan, can
be accomplished "at comparatively low cost" and in far less time
than a sea-level project would require.

Fourth. Between 1904 and 1966 we invested more than
$4,889,051,000 on the Panama Canal and the Armed Forces
defending it.

Fifth. Through our obsession with the construction of a canal
of so-called sea-level design, we are losing control of the Canal
Zone and Panama Canal through a policy of surrender.

Sixth. If we cannot hold the canal which we built, own, and
have maintained at our expense and over which we are sovereign,
the United States will be completely driven from the Isthmus and
Panama will become another Cuba.

The time has come, Mr. Speaker, for a prompt reappraisal

by our Government of its policy of surrender at Panama, for the assertion of our just rights in the Canal Zone, and for the major increase of capacity and operational improvement of the Panama Canal along the lines of the program outlined in the "Minority Report" previously mentioned.

*   *   *   *

Near East Crisis Emphasizes Peril At Panama

Mr. Speaker, in speaking bluntly as I have done today, I have so spoken because of the gravity of the situation at Panama demands such treatment, especially as regards the transcendent question of maintaining our full sovereignty over the Canal Zone. The basic question in the proposed surrender of our sovereignty there is not U.S. control over the Panama Canal versus Panamanian control but American control versus Communist control. In the Near East, Egypt, with Soviet collaboration, not only denies transit of the Suez Canal to some countries but also threatens to block that waterway completely if any move is made contrary to the dictates of Nasser and the Soviet. These facts emphasize with greater force than anything I can say about the peril at Panama.

Except for the bold and truculent support given to Dictator Nasser by the Soviet Government he would never dare to challenge the free world or to threaten it. If Soviet power is permitted to dominate the Panama Canal then every country in Latin-America will be lost to Red revolutionary power and the control of two strategic canals will enable communism to sweep over the world with its long continued and avowed policy of bringing all nations into the Soviet orbit.

How blind are those who will not see: The United States must maintain its exclusive sovereign rights, power, and authority over the Canal Zone and Panama Canal undiluted and in perpetuity.

In order that those studying this address may have the benefit of significant parts of the previously indicated booklet and certain other documents, I quote them and my commentary on the "majority report" as parts of my remarks:

[From the Center for Strategic Studies, Georgetown University, Washington, D.C., Special Report Series No. 3, March 1967]

Panama Canal Issues and Treaty Talk— Part II—Minority Report

(Part two is a report by a minority of the Panel. In our consideration of Panama Canal problems we are unwilling to be limited by the joint announcement of Presidents Johnson and Robles on September 24, 1965. We do not accept the view that a presidential statement that purports to abrogate a treaty which has been constitutionally ratified and to relinquish sovereign control over legally acquired territory of the United States should be allowed to serve as a definitive guideline for this study or to block a full and openminded consideration of Canal problems. Our analysis dealing more broadly with those problems therefore leads us to some conclusions different from those of the preceding report. — Dr. Donald M. Dozer and Vice Admiral T. G. W. Settle, U. S. N. (Ret.)

Historical Analysis

Panama, despite its small population of only 1.2 million, enjoys a status of singular importance because of its geographical position astride the Isthmus connecting the continents of North and South America. At the same time, its location makes it a focus of envy of the predatory communist nations that are working constantly to seize and control it. The Isthmus is one of the great strategic and military centers of the world.

Panama's independence was protected by the United States under the Hay-Bunau-Varilla treaty from 1903 to 1939, but since World War II its independent status has been compromised by a succession of crises, some fomented by communist-oriented agitators and some by surrenders to Panama by the United States of important rights, power, and authority, which is indispensable to effective management of the Canal and to safeguarding U.S. interests there. The global implications of these mounting crises in Panama, aimed at wresting control of the Canal from the United States, may be seen in the coincidence of events there with those in the Suez Canal, in South Africa, and in Vietnam, all directed toward gaining control of the strategic waterways of the world. The preservation of the sovereign control of the United States over the Canal Zone and the Panama Canal is more vital to this nation than victory in Vietnam. The further forfeiture of that control will constitute a major surrender by the United States and may be expected to trigger communist takeovers of governments in Latin America.

The United States was acknowledged in 1903 by all the maritime nations to have an international mandate to construct, maintain, operate, sanitate, and protect a canal across the American Isthmus for the benefit of world commerce. It chose Panama over Nicaragua as the site of the Canal because of its superiority and because Panama offered as an inducement a grant of sovereign control over a canal zone and other concessions outside the zone which were indispensable to the discharge of that mandate. These were embodied in the Hay-Bunau-Varilla Treaty of 1903, which granted "in perpetuity" to the United States "all the rights, power and authority . . . which the United States would possess and exercise if it were the sovereign of the territory . . . to the entire exclusion of the exercise by the Republic of Panama of any such sovereign rights, power or authority" (Article III). This article, which still remains legally in full force and effect, granted the United States the sovereign control which has been demonstrated ever since as essential to enable it to discharge its canal responsibilities. It was intended to remove "in perpetuity" any possibility of claims against the United States for the exercise by Panama or any other nation of extraterritorial rights in the Zone. Panama gave the United States these extensive rights "in perpetuity" in return for the obligation of the United States to operate the canal in perpetuity and to guarantee its independence. Just as Panama committed itself to granting to the United States in perpetuity a strip of its own land for building, operating, and maintaining an interoceanic canal the United States committed itself also in perpetuity to operate and maintain the canal. Panama thus gained an advantage which she would forfeit only at her cost and peril.

It should be noted that the Hay-Bunau-Varilla treaty was constitutionally ratified by both Panama and the United States and that when Panama adopted its first constitution in February 1904 it expressly ratified all the measures that had been enacted by the Provisional Government including the Hay-Bunau-Varilla treaty.

In implementing the treaty the United States proceeded to acquire outright ownership of all land and other property in the Canal Zone by purchase from the individual owners. The rights exercised by the United States in the Canal Zone are derived therefore from both the grant from the government of Panama and purchase from the individual property owners.

The total cost of the acquisition of the Canal Zone, as reported by the Deputy Secretary of the Army on March 31, 1964, is as follows:

Original payment, 1904 (treaty of 1903).........	$10,000,000
Annuity, 1913-1963, (treaties of 1903, 1936, 1955)	30,150,000
Property transfers:	
In Panama City and Colon, 1943..............	11,759,956
Water system in Panama City and Colon.......	669,226
Under treaty of 1955......................	22,260,500
Colombia (1922).............................	25,000,000
Compagnie Nouvelle du Canal de Panama (1904) .	40,000,000
Private titles, stocks, and claims...............	4,728,889
Total...................................	144,568,571

The principal objectives of the Isthmian Canal policy of the United States, as historically evolved, have been to construct, maintain, and operate the best possible type of canal at the best possible site for the transit of vessels of commerce and war of all nations on terms of equality as provided by treaty and to do so at the lowest possible cost of construction, maintenance, operation, sanitation, and protection. The United States has traditionally considered the Panama Canal as vital to her security and commercial interests and has operated it on a self-sustaining basis.

For more than ten years the United States has been enmeshed in crisis diplomacy with Panama and has responded with one concession after another, each of which has been followed by new and greater demands from Panama. While retaining the responsibility, embodied not only in the Hay-Bunau-Varilla Treaty with Panama but also in treaties with Great Britain (Hay-Pauncefote, 1901) and Colombia (Thomson-Urrutia, 1914-1922), the United States has progressively relinquished its authority in the Canal Zone under pressure from communist-led demonstrations and demagogic Panamanian politicians thus furthering the long-range communist objective of gaining control of the strategic waterways of the world.

To this pressure the United States has responded only with concession after concession. In the treaty of 1955, it increased the annuity to Panama by $1,500,000, to make a total annual payment of $1,930,000. At the same time it gave to Panama approximately $25 million worth of miscellaneous parcels of lands, relinquished its treaty responsibility for sanitation in the cities of Panama and Colon, and turned over to Panama the railroad terminals, passenger stations, and freight yards in those cities, all without compensation.

Over and above the financial benefits which the Panamanians derive from the Canal enterprise they have received from the United States between 1946 and 1964 a total of $128 million in financial aid or more than $100 for every man, woman, and child in the country. This aid from the United States exceeds the total amount given to any other Central American country except Guatemala and the per capita amount given to any other Central American country except Costa Rica.

In return for the concessions which the United States made to Panama in the treaties of 1936 and 1955 Panama promised to "strengthen further the bonds of friendship and cooperation" with the United States to promote mutual understanding and friendship of her people with the United States. Panama has not fulfilled her part of this bargain. Meanwhile, the concessions made to her are increasingly seen to have been unwise, for they appear as part of a plan to wrest control of the Canal from the United States through piecemeal erosion. The agitation and demonstrations in Panama against the treaty position of the United States in the Zone, if continued, can only result in driving the United States from the Isthmus. Panama's repeated thrusts are directed toward the total liquidation of United States sovereignty and control over the Panama Canal. In December 1958 Panama took the bold step of proclaiming the extension of its territorial waters to a twelve-mile limit thus encompassing within its own territory the area beyond the three-mile limit of canal operations at both ends of the Canal Zone which was stipulated in the treaty of 1903. Panama thus established a legal basis for bottling up the United States in the Zone.

Key Issues

The key Isthmian Canal issues facing the United States are: (1) whether the United States should insist upon preserving its existing treaty rights, power, and authority over the Canal Zone in order that it may adequately discharge its treaty responsibility for the efficient maintenance, operation, sanitation, and protection of the Panama Canal for the benefit of its own commerce and the commerce of the world and that it may at the same time defend and protect its own security interests and those of other nations of the western hemisphere, and (2) whether, because of the approaching traffic saturation of Canal capacity, the United States should construct additional Canal facilities required to meet increased traffic demands. This latter question has reopened the old debate as to the advisability of constructing (1) a so-called sea-level canal across the Isthmus, possibly with nuclear excavation, or (2) an alternate canal at a site other than the site of the existing canal. The United States has allowed itself to be impaled on the dilemma as to how far it can go in acceding to Panama's demands while retaining the control necessary to discharge its treaty obligations and protect its own vital interests in the Canal Zone. The problems of the Canal, which involve primarily matters of engineering and operation, have been allowed to become seriously intertwined with matters of politics and diplomacy, and the advocates of a sea-level canal, taking advantage of the resulting confusion, are again pushing their favorite project.

The United States has been maneuvered into its current negotiations with Panama by the blackmail tactics of Panama, aided and abetted by communist conspiratorial forces and by successive administrations in Washington. In this situation whatever bargaining advantage still rests with the United States is further weakened by its virtual dependence upon a satisfactory settlement with Panama and by the pressure being exerted by the Panamanian government for a speedy termination of the current treaty negotiations due to the political climate in Panama. In all the negotiations which the United States has carried on with Panama since 1936 it has never, except on a few slight occasions, required any reciprocal concessions by Panama. All that Panama seems to be expected to offer is a cessation of demonstrations and mob action against the United States, which it seems to be able to turn on and off at will. In addition, in the propaganda campaign for a sea-level canal among special interest groups in the United States, Panama has been supplied with a lever which it is shrewdly using to maximum advantage. These are Panama's only negotiation assets. Hence, the conditions for reciprocally satisfactory negotiation are lacking, and for this reason the current negotiations are stalemated. To put them on a proper basis it is necessary that the United States recover its position of bargaining strength and that Panama be made conscious of its international obligations as an avowedly responsible member of the American and international community.

Conclusions

The United States therefore should:

(1) *Terminate immediately its present negotiations with Panama while holding Panama to strict accountability for respecting and enforcing its treaty obligations for the maintenance of law and order;*

(2) *Withdraw any and all arrangements for shared management of the Canal.* Panama does not possess the skilled managerial and operating personnel required to handle the Canal. Moreover, as a country of mercurial politics it lacks the stable government necessary to discharge this responsibility to world commerce. Since 1930 Panama has undergone five unconstitutional changes of heads of state. Little comfort can be gained from examining the backgrounds of opposition leaders in Panama today or the extent of communist influence among the youth of that country.

(3) *Reassert its position of sovereign control over the Canal and the Canal Zone, which has been dangerously weakened by action of Presidents Eisenhower, Kennedy, and Johnson.* As a symbol of its sovereign control it should allow only the United States flag to be flown in the Zone. The successes which the communists have already achieved in extending the area of their control, as notably in the case of Cuba, render it imperative that the United States maintain all its treaty rights, power, and authority over the Canal.

(4) *Insist upon Panamanian recognition of the full force and validity of the 1903 Treaty allowing, however, an adjustment of the annuity provided in that treaty;*

(5) *As a necessary condition to the resumption of treaty negotiations, require that Panama agree to a revocation of certain major concessions made to her in the treaties of 1936 and 1955, which appear in perspective to have been only stepping stones to ultimate conquest of the Canal from the United States;*

(6) *Insist upon receiving from Panama in perpetuity the entire watershed of the Chagres River, thus enabling the United States, within the terms of the Treaty of 1903, to proceed with the modernization of the Canal and the enlargement of its traffic capacity with a secure water supply.* It is important to note that the United States did not insist upon receiving a canal zone wider than ten miles in 1903 because it was given in the Hay-Bunau-Varilla treaty the right of eminent domain in Panama for all necessary canal purposes. The recommendation that the Canal Zone should be widened to include the entire watershed of the Chagres River was made initially by General Clarence R.

Edwards while commanding the United States Army in the
Canal Zone in 1915-1917. The United States surrendered the
right of eminent domain in Panama in the Treaty of 1936 but
now needs control over the entire Chagres River basin outside the
Zone for the operation of the Canal. Only in this way can it
prevent the burning of timber on the headwaters of the Chagres
River by irresponsible *campesinos* and the resulting soil erosion
which limits the water available for canal operations. The
advantages to Panama from this additional grant can and should
be convincingly demonstrated to Panamanians by their own
political leaders.

Panama owes her national existence to the Canal enterprise,
and from it she has derived, and will derive as long as the United
States remains in sovereign control, tremendous economic benefits, which have given her one of the highest standards of living in
all Latin America.

(7) *Abandon plans for the digging of a new canal, whether by
nuclear or by conventional methods.* The Governor of the Canal
Zone reported in 1931: "Considering the low cost of providing
water for additional lockages by pumping, it is apparent that the
ultimate capacity of the Panama Canal with locks is unlimited
and may be increased to any amount desired by constructing
additional locks and installing the necessary pumping equipment," thus ultimately envisaging a third, perhaps a fourth, and
even a fifth set of locks.

A sea-level canal project derives advantages from its glamorous appeal and from the grandiose vision it creates of a
Panama strait comparable to the Straits of Magellan. But it
should be emphasized that the term sea-level canal is a mis-
nomer; because of the differential in tides on the Pacific and the
Caribbean sides of the Isthmus, with maximum ranges of 22 feet
on the Pacific and only about 22 inches on the Caribbean, even a
so-called sea-level canal would necessarily have to be a tidal-lock
canal. The regulating works for tidal control, as well as the high
dikes required to divert flood waters in a sea-level canal, would
make such a canal as vulnerable to nuclear attack in wartime as
the present lock canal, in fact more so because of the greater
length and depth of the cut which will be necessary.

John Frank Stevens, Basic Architect of the Panama Canal

Senator Strom Thurmond, Republican, South Carolina
Defender of the Panama Canal

Congressman Daniel J. Flood, Democrat, Pennsylvania
Defender of the Panama Canal

Gatun locks looking southward over Gatun Lake

Gatun locks looking northward toward Limon Bay

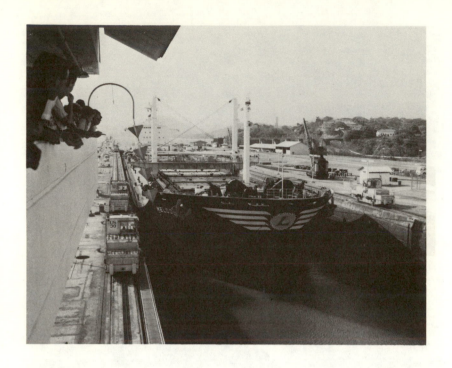

Top: Miraflores locks looking northward over Miraflores Lake toward the bottleneck Pedro Miguel locks
Bottom: Miraflores locks looking southward

Top and bottom: Two views of Miraflores locks in operation, looking northward over Miraflores Lake toward the bottleneck Pedro Miguel locks.

Large vessel southbound in Gaillard cut, opposite Gold Hill

There is no substantial, evidential support for the assertion that a sea-level canal would require fewer supporting facilities and administrative procedures than the present Canal. On the contrary it seems highly probable that since a sea-level canal would be more susceptible to slides and will present unprecedentedly large maintenance problems it will require larger supporting facilities and administrative staffs. Moreover, the expense of digging a new canal at any site different from that of the existing Canal must take into consideration the following costs, among others:

a. Purchase of the right-of-way;

b. Indemnity of Panama for leaving the present site;

c. Purchase price for real estate at the new site; and

d. Construction at the new site of new facilities which are already constructed and being used at the existing Canal, including harbors and docks, drydocks, shops, fueling and oil storage facilities, industrial plants, storehouses, towns with water, fuel, and electric current, roads, parks, schools, police stations, dams, reservoirs, electric power plants, telephone systems, sanitation systems, hospitals, defense installations, and many others.

Terminal Lake-Third Locks Plan

(8) *Proceed with the improvement of the existing Canal in accordance with the Terminal Lake-Third Locks Plan in order to provide necessary additional transit capacity in the Canal.* This plan grew out of wartime experience after 1941 which disclosed the following as principal Canal problems:

a. The traffic bottleneck at Pedro Miguel locks and lack of a summit-level traffic reservoir at the Pacific end.

b. Double handling of vessels at the separated Pacific locks.

c. Effects of fog in Gaillard Cut on Canal capacity and operations.

d. Lockage surges in the Gaillard Cut caused by operation of the Pedro Miguel Locks.

e. Limited operating range of the water level in Gatun Lake (87-82 feet).

f. Navigational hazards in Gaillard Cut due to its narrow width (300 feet minimum bottom width).

g. Inadequate dimensions of the locks for the largest vessels (110 feet by 1,000 feet by 41 feet).

To overcome these difficulties the Terminal Lake-Third Locks plan was proposed and was authoritatively recognized as supplying the best operational canal practicable of achievement. It called for elimination of Pedro Miguel Locks, the consolidation of all Pacific locks near Miraflores, the creation of a summit-level anchorage in the Pacific end of the Canal to match that at Gatun, and elevating the summit water level to its optimum height of 92 feet. It will thus provide summit-level navigation from Gatun to Miraflores with obvious operational benefits including reduced transit time for vessels and an anchorage area immediately north of the Miraflores locks. This plan, as contrasted with the sea-level plan, will not empty Gatún Lake, but will raise it from 85 to 92 feet and will provide ample water supply for the operation of the Canal for many years to come.

This plan was recommended by the Governor of the Canal Zone to the Secretary of War for comprehensive investigation, was supported by maritime interests, and won the support of the President as a post-war project. The Governor of the Canal Zone, however, in his report to the Secretary of War warned that there remained advocates of a sea-level canal who would oppose "unjustifiably" any major improvement of the existing Canal on the grounds that it would delay the adoption of their sea-level scheme.

The advent of the atomic bomb near the end of World War II generated a new concern for Canal security.

As a result, the new Governor of the Canal Zone secured authorization to conduct a comprehensive investigation of the means of increasing the capacity "and security" of the Panama Canal to meet the needs of interoceanic commerce "and national defense", including a restudy of the 1939 Third Locks Project (Public Law 280, 79th Congress). In the hearings he approved the terminal lake proposal in principle as the proper form for modernizing the existing Canal.

The advocates of a sea-level route, according to their own statements, used "security" as their rallying cry and, ignoring money costs, tried to push through their scheme, which, in its modern form, called for the building of a sea-level canal near the approximate route of the present Canal and crossing it several times, a tidal lock, many miles of dams for flood control reservoirs on both sides of the projected canal, and four diversion channels.

There was a determined drive by those who would benefit to secure its authorization, including the manufacture of heavy earthmoving machinery, dredging combines, contractors, and a limited group of engineers. But their proposal failed to receive Presidential approval and was not accepted by the Congress.

It was estimated at that time that the digging of a sea-level canal along the existing route would involve channel excavation of approximately one billion cubic yards of material. By comparison the total channel excavation for the present Canal, including the usable excavation performed by the French, was approximately 275 million cubic yards or only one-fourth as much. Questions were raised at the time by nuclear warfare experts whether a sea-level canal would actually prove to be less vulnerable to atomic attack than a summit-level canal.

In 1957 the House of Representatives authorized the appointment of an independent Board of Consultants on Isthmian Canal Studies to investigate plans for the operation and improvement of the Panama Canal. This Board, initially composed of six experts drawn from private life, presented its report in June 1960 (86th Congress, 2d Session, *House Report No. 1960*). The Board estimated the cost of the Terminal Lake-Third Locks project, on which $75 million had been spent between 1940 and 1942 and which had been shown by World War II experience to be necessary, at almost $1,021 million. This estimate was extravagant, however, because it was based upon locks of excessive dimensions, 200 feet by 1500 feet by 55 feet whereas the original Third-Locks Project called for locks of 140 feet by 1200 feet by 50 feet. The Board estimated the initial cost of a sea-level canal with regulating structures at $2,537 million, not including diplomatic costs, which would undoubtedly be huge.

They concluded that the present Canal, if modernized in accordance with the "consolidated third-locks" design in order to accommodate vessels with a beam of 132 feet, "will have fully adequate capacity to meet the demands of traffic beyond the year 2000," taking into consideration a report by the Stanford Research Institute that commercial freight traffic through the Canal would more than double in tonnage by the year 2000.

With reference to the proposal of a sea-level canal, the Board reported that the fixed charges of such a canal are "very high and would commence with the start of the enormous construction job. If started now, these fixed charges would commence decades before the volume of traffic, even with increased rates, could absorb them. Hence a subsidy would be required to meet a heavy deficit over a period of many years. . . . We are doubtful," they added, "if any reasonable plan to construct a sea-level canal in the Canal Zone could be carried through without serious danger of a long interruption to traffic at the time of cutover from the present lock canal." The Board was also "extremely doubtful of the stability of the slopes resulting from the construction of a sea-level canal." "In our opinion," they concluded, "slides of the first magnitude could easily result from the use of such slopes." As a further objection, they pointed out, the differential in tides on the Atlantic and the Pacific "would at times cause currents in the channel up to 4.5 knots in a sea-level canal without tidal-regulating structures. This flow, combined with currents caused by flood and intermingling of fresh and salt water, would produce currents up to 7 knots in certain places."

The Terminal Lake-Third Locks proposal makes possible a maximum utilization of all the work done thus far on the Panama Canal, including the Third Locks project between 1940 and 1942 and the continuing work of widening and deepening the channel, which has been going forward since 1960. All that remains is to construct larger locks in the present Canal. This proposal, calling only for an enlargement of existing facilities within the Canal Zone, does not require a new treaty with Panama but is covered by existing treaties—a paramount consideration because of current diplomatic difficulties with Panama.

The canal facility that is required at Panama is a two-way ship channel across the Isthmus with a traffic reservoir and ample lock capacity at both ends of the canal. The two-way ship channel is complete except for about three miles in Gaillard Cut, and the reservoirs and lock capacity will be provided under the Terminal Lake-Third Locks plan. This plan will necessitate a minimal additional expense, will require no new treaty negotiations, and will enable the Canal to accommodate all but approximately two percent of the vessels in world shipping well into the twenty-first century.

Objection to this simple, obvious, and economic solution has been raised that it would be only an interim solution, but all transportation systems are interim solutions. What is needed is one based upon the realities of the problem of economic transit across the American Isthmus. The evidence is conclusive that a lake-lock canal can be jusified on a business basis whereas a sea-level project cannot be. If the time should ever come when a modernized Panama Canal with a two-way ship channel in the summit level equipped with ample lock capacity at each end becomes insufficient, then something more could be done. In any event, such a time is so far away that it should not be allowed to influence current decisions.

*   *   *   *   *

We now have a fine canal.

We know it will work.

We know how to operate it.

We know how to enlarge it from time to time as necessity requires.

We have a treaty with Panama which enables us to operate it and control it, though this treaty is now being abrogated by executive fiat.

We are losing control of the Panama Canal through a policy of retreat and through our obsession with the construction of a canal of sea-level design which weakens our bargaining position.

If we cannot control the Canal which we now own, we may be forced entirely out of the canal business in Central America.

If this happens, who will control this priceless interoceanic utility? Who will operate it to serve the needs of world commerce?

Public Law 88-60, 88th Congress, S. 2701, Sept. 22, 1964, 78 Stat. 990.

An act to provide for an investigation and study to determine a site for the construction of a sea level canal connecting the Atlantic and Pacific Oceans.

Be it enacted by the Senate and House of Representatives of the United States of America in Congress assembled, That the President is authorized to appoint a Commission to be composed of five men from private life, to make a full and complete investigation and study, including necessary on-site surveys, and considering national defense, foreign relations, intercoastal shipping, interoceanic shipping, and such other matters as they may determine to be important, for the purpose of determining the feasibility of, and the most suitable site for, the construction of a sea level canal connecting the Atlantic and Pacific Oceans; the best means of constructing such a canal, whether by conventional or nuclear excavation, and the estimated cost thereof. The President shall designate as Chairman one of the members of the Commission.

Sec. 2. The Commission is authorized to utilize the facilities of any department, agency, or instrumentality of the executive branch of the United States Government, and to obtain such services as it deems necessary in accordance with the provisions of section 15 of the Act of August 2, 1946 (5 U.S.C. 55a).

Sec. 3. The Commission shall report to the President for transmittal to Congress on July 31, 1965, with respect to its progress, and each year thereafter until the completion of its duties. The President shall submit such recommendations to the Congress as he deems advisable. The Commission shall continue until the President determines that its duties are completed, but not later than June 30, 1968.

Sec. 4. There are hereby authorized to be appropriated such

amounts as may be necessary to carry out the provisions of this Act, not to exceed $17,500,000.

Approved September 22, 1964.

Legislative History

House Report No. 1706 (Comm. on Merchant Marine & Fisheries).

Senate Report No. 968 (Comm. on Commerce).

Congressional Record, Vol. 110 (1964): Mar. 30: Considered and passed Senate. Aug. 12: Considered in House. Sept. 1: Considered and passed House, amended. Sept. 8: Senate concurred in House amendments.

Panama Canal Issues and Treaty Talks

Early in January 1964 a crisis in U.S.-Panamanian relations, which had been brewing for some time, suddenly assumed major proportions, when violence erupted at the Panama Canal Zone. Ostensibly, the cause of the disturbance involved the raising of the flags of the United States of America and the Republic of Panama in front of the Balboa High School in the Zone. The incident, however, had its tap root deep in the problems related to U.S. control and operations of the Panama Canal, and the status of the Canal Zone, which had been the focal point of the bilateral relations between the two countries for over 60 years.

Because the Canal looms large in the complex network of world commerce and vitally influences the relations of the United States not only with Panama, but also with other countries of Latin America, effective ways of dealing with the major stresses within U.S.-Panamanian relations must be developed.

The United States has agreed, at Panama's insistence, to negotiate new treaty arrangements. These will deal with the issues of sovereignty over the Canal Zone, continued operation and administration of the Panama Canal, its economic benefits for the Republic of Panama, and the possibilities of a new sea-level canal. The challenging task of finding common grounds of agreement between the United States and Panama will demand a high measure of statesmanship on the part of the leaders of those countries.

The following report is a study of basic issues that now divide the United States and Panama and that are highlighted in current negotiations. Since the United States must be concerned with present and future canal requirements, with the welfare of Panama and the demands of world commerce, and with its own security and that of the western hemisphere, it seeks broad-based agreements that will not jeopardize these interests.

Among the key Isthmian canal questions are:

How can Panama's insistence on sovereignty over the Panama Canal and Canal Zone be reconciled with the U.S. claim that Panama has neither the resources nor capacity to manage, operate, and defend the Canal efficiently?

Should the present Canal be improved or should a new canal be built in Panama to handle the increased navigation and traffic demands that are expected to reach critical proportions early in the next century?

If a new canal is constructed should it be by conventional or nuclear means?

If nuclear excavation is chosen, what arrangements would be necessary in light of the Limited Nuclear Test Ban Treaty?

What compensation should Panama receive for either an improved or a new canal facility?

If agreement cannot be reached with Panama, should the United States build a new canal across Colombia or at some other location?

All these questions are subject to debate. Differences of opinion may be found within the United States and within Panama.

Because the interests at stake are so important and the progress of negotiations has been so limited, the Center for Strategic Studies invited a group of practicing experts, with diverse views on Panama's situation, to make an independent investigation of the issues and to draw up conclusions, which they feel would help resolve the unsettled questions.

The Panel, under the chairmanship of Ambassador Joseph S. Farland, found it necessary to include both a majority and a minority report in its final document in order to give a fair representation of the views held by the Panel members. Some of the conclusions have also been divided between majority and minority viewpoints. It is intended that the material presented within the study should provide scope for criticism from those who are concerned with the stimulation of progress in Panama-U.S. relations.

A special note of appreciation is due to Jeremiah O'Leary and Sheldon Z. Kaplan for their assistance in preparation of the report.

Arleigh Burke,
Director.

Members of the Panel

Joseph S. Farland, Chairman, U.S. Ambassador to Dominican Republic, 1957-1960; to Panama, 1960-1963.

Major General William A. Carter, USA (Ret.), Deputy Director, Project Analysis Division, Inter-American Development Bank; Governor of the Canal Zone, 1960-1962.

Jules Davids, Professor of American Diplomatic History, Georgetown University.

Donald Marquand Dozer, Professor of Latin American History, University of California, Santa Barbara, California; State Department, Division of Research for American Republics and the Historical Division, 1944-1956.

Eleanor Lansing Dulles, Professor of Government, Georgetown University; State Department, 1942-1962.

Victor O. Folsom, Vice President and General Counsel, United Fruit Company.

Major General K. D. Nichols, USA (Ret.), Consulting engineer; District Engineer, Manhattan District, 1942-1947; General Manager, A.E.C., 1953-1955.

Covey T. Oliver, Professor of International Law, University of Pennsylvania; U.S. Ambassador to Colombia, 1964-1966.

Vice Admiral T. G. W. Settle, USN (Ret.), Formerly

Commander, Amphibious Forces, U.S. Pacific Fleet; service in Caribbean, Asiatic and European waters, including transportation, shipping and navigational affairs.

Conclusions of the Panel [1]

For over sixty years, from November 18, 1903 to September 24, 1965, from Theodore Roosevelt's administration through the aftermath of the riots of 1964, U.S. policy toward Panama and the Panama Canal was based upon three major concepts: a) that the United States has sovereignty within the Canal Zone; b) that the rights obtained were held in perpetuity; and c) that the Canal tolls if at all possible would not be increased.

President Johnson's joint announcement with the President of Panama on September 24, 1965 publicly altered this basic policy position. By this statement, the Johnson administration agreed to abrogate the 1903 treaty, to relinquish its rights of sovereignty over the Zone, to place a term upon the contractual arrangements and tacitly to increase tolls.

With the exception of Dr. Dozer and Vice Admiral Settle, whose views will be found in the Minority Report, the members of the Panel have not directed their attention toward the merit of this policy change, but rather, because it was a Presidential announcement, believe that the position is now established as a fait accompli. Consequently, it is within this frame of reference that the following observations and conclusions are set forth:

1. The negotiation of new arrangements between the Republic of Panama and the United States were delayed by both parties in varying degrees during the initial phases of the talks. Delays were in part caused by the 1964 transition to a new administration in the Republic of Panama, the new administration's attempt to find financial backing for construction of a new canal independent of the United States, and its subsequent unsuccessful attempts to obtain support from other Latin American governments for an increase in Canal tolls. The United

---

[1] Some other conclusions prepared by a Panel minority from its different analysis of Canal issues and treaty talks will be found in Part Two.

States was responsible for delays caused by a fruitless argument over semantics and by inadequate staffing during the early months of the talks. Although these delays, with the exception of Panama's search for support of toll increases, took place prior to the spring of 1965, they cause the loss of valuable negotiating time.

2. There is now an urgent need for the U.S. and Panamanian negotiators to reach agreement on the terms of the new treaties. Thi... .... resulting primarily from pressures ....ama. Whereas it will be decades .... :omes technically and economically ....nal issues are certain to become ....anian politics, especially with Pan- ....scheduled for May, 1968, and with ....r in advance. Unsettled Canal issues ....r deterioration of relations between ....na.

...........oach of the two governments should ....aneous consideration of the three ....nd status-of-forces agreement; b) a ....eaty together with its amendments; ....ew canal or improve the present one. ....negotiation ought to be completed and ....approval in each nation by the fall of .... p may exclude waiting for the completion of all details of the engineering and economic studies now under way.

4. The security of the United States and the security of the western hemisphere demand that the defense of the present and any future Isthmian Canal shall continue to rest with the United States for the duration of the final treaty agreements that are negotiated.

5. Although a new or improved canal facility across the Isthmus will be needed early in the next century because of increased user demands and changes in shipbuilding technology, the design and time of construction should be left flexible in the treaties.

France. *Institut nationa...*
économiques. Recens...
1962. 1964. (Card 2)
CONT...
Loiret.—3.1. Nord: Nord, P...
Moselle, Meuse, Moselle, Vos...
4.3. Franche-Comté: Doubs...
fort.—5.1. Basse-Normandie...
la Loire: Loire-Atlantiq...
Vendée.—5.3. Bretagne: C...
Morbihan.—6.1. Limousin:...
Auvergne: Allier, Cantal,...
Charentes: Charente, Cha...
7.2. Aquitaine: Dordogne, ...

6. Though the Republic of Panama seems technically to be the best place for a future canal facility, the United States should not abandon the right to approach other countries for possible canal location in the event that future political conditions exclude the project from Panama.

7. The U.S. nuclear testing program related to canal excavation technology is proceeding too slowly if such a technique is to be developed in time for competitive consideration with conventional excavation techniques. If new negotiations among signatories of the Limited Nuclear Test Ban Treaty are required to permit adequate testing, they should be initiated at once. For the present, the United States should not hamper its testing program by making its interpretation of the treaty unnecessarily strict.

8. Panama should receive added economic benefits from the present or any alternative canal within its borders. Any increase should be based upon an equitable allocation of financial return from canal operations. Though the economic impact on users must be the primary concern when formulating the increase, the United States and other users must fully consider that Panama's principal natural resource is its strategic location for canal purposes, and that canal tolls have not been permanently raised since the canal was placed in operation.

9. The past failure of the U.S. government to make a persuasive case for the benefits Panama and other Latin American nations receive from U.S. operation of the Canal has laid a basis for persistent criticism of the United States. Therefore, the present U.S. administration should immediately take measures to impress upon the people of the hemisphere the multiple benefits received by them from successful U.S. operation of the Canal.

Commentary on Majority Report—Panama Canal Issues and Treaty Talks, Center for Strategic Studies, Georgetown University, Washington, D.C., March 1967

Page 4, Lines 5 to 8

"How can Panama's insistence on sovereignty over the

Panama Canal and Canal Zone be reconciled with the U.S. claim that Panama has neither the resources nor capacity to manage, operate, and defend the Canal efficiently?"

Comment

This is the first in a series of "key Isthmian Canal questions" listed in the Preface of the booklet on *Panama Canal Issues and Treaty Talks*. The Preface, as is a whole, is not directed toward inquiring into the merits of the cession of Canal Zone sovereignty by the United States to Panama but toward acceptance of the September 24, 1965, announcement that the proposed new treaty would recognize Panama's sovereignty over the Canal Zone. The canal sovereignty question should not be subject to debate and the quoted statement, in effect, shows the fallacy in the Panamian contention.

Moreover, as used, the term "sovereignty" is an over simplification, for the meaning of the 1903 Treaty as written is so clear that there is no doubt at all. What is really indicated is cession back to Panama of the Canal Zone, which signifies separation of the Canal Zone Government from the Panama Canal Company—an inherent impossibility.

Page 7, Paragraph 3

"... the members of the Panel have not directed their attention toward the merit of this policy change (Joint statement of September 24, 1965), but rather, because it was a Presidential announcement, believe that the position is now established as a *fait accompli*."

Comment

No Presidential statement purporting to abrogate a duly ratified treaty and to cede a Constitutionally acquired territorial possession of the United States is a *fait accompli* but only the expression of the President and the advisers on whom he depended. The Senate is a part of the treaty making department of our government and the Congress is the ultimate authority in matters of foreign policy and implementing appropriations. U.S. sovereignty in perpetuity over the Canal Zone was acquired by treaty pursuant to law authorizing the acquisition of its control in perpetuity and the Congress has not authorized its cession either to Panama or to any other country or agency. It would be just as logical to contend that a *fait accompli* would be created by a mere agreement between the Presidents of the United States and Mexico for the cession of our great Southwest back to Mexico. Any such proposed treaty to be effected would have to be ratified by the U.S. Senate; and implemented by the Congress for any appropriations involved.

Page 8, Paragraph 3

"3. The negotiating approach of the two governments should continue to be the simultaneous consideration of the three treaties: (a) the base-rights and status-of-forces agreement; (b) a replacement for the 1903 treaty together with its amendments; and (c) an option to build a new canal or improve the present one."

Comment

The linking of these three treaties is unfortunate, for it weakens our bargaining position. The major improvement of the existing canal is authorized by existing treaty provision and does not require the negotiation of a new one. A new canal of sea level design, either in the Canal Zone or in Panama, is not covered by existing treaty and would require the negotiation of a new one to determine the specific conditions for its construction.

We should not allow current obsession with the idea of a canal at sea level and an administrative policy of surrender to cause the United States to lose control of the Canal Zone, which is so indispensable for the protection and defense of the present one. To illustrate, in January 1964 the mob, had it not been restrained, could have sabotaged or destroyed the canal itself. Moreover, as the Panama Canal is the greatest symbol of power and prestige of the United States throughout Latin-America and a key target for Red conquest of the Caribbean, the surrender of the Canal Zone could actuate a series of revolutions in the Western Hemisphere. Also, its loss would make a serious impact on other focal strategic areas: Southeast Asia, Suez Canal-Red Sea route to the Indian Ocean, Southern Africa and the sea lanes around the Cape of Good Hope.

Page 9, Paragraph 8, Lines 1 to 4

"8. Panama should receive added economic benefits from the present or any alternative canal within its borders. Any increase should be based upon an *equitable allocation* of financial return from canal operations."

Comment

More than $100,000,000 annually through purchases and employment are now injected into Panama's economy from Canal Zone sources. What is meant by "equitable allocation." The Panama Canal, under law, is required to operate on a self-sustaining basis. As any increase of benefits to Panama from Canal sources would have to be borne by users who pay tolls or by U.S. taxpayers, the Canal should be disassociated from any welfare program from Panama and operated on a strict business-like basis, in which event, as at present, that country is substantially rewarded.

Page 9, Paragraph 8, Lines 6 to 8

". . . users must fully consider that Panama's principal *natural resource* is its strategic location for canal purposes. . . ."

Comment

Brigands and highwaymen through history have habitually ganged up at the crossroads of commerce. As to Panama's "principal natural resource" being its strategic location, this is also its greatest danger, for its territory is coveted by predatory powers bent on world domination. Panama's security as a free country depends absolutely on the presence of the United States in the Canal Zone. Our negotiators ought to stress this fact and not commit a grave diplomatic blunder because of a lack of realistic thinking by our own government. Panamanian negotiators have, in large measure, accepted and presented the arguments and slogans of the mob. Our own negotiators should present the realism of wise and objective statesmen and not allow themselves to be brainwashed.

Page 7 Line 19

". . . United States as the sole guarantor of these provisions (Hay-Pauncefote Treaty)."

Comment

This should be strengthened by adding: "which responsibility for the 'regulation and management' of an interoceanic canal the United States assumed as a mandate for civilization and under which mandate our country, at its own expense, constructed the Canal and has ever since maintained and operated it."

Page 10, Last Sentence

"For the rejection of the sea level plan at that time (1906) the new Chief Engineer, John F. Stevens, was partly responsible, because he found no advocate of a sea level canal among the engineering force on the Isthmus. . . ."

Comment

Historically, this statement is misleading as well as inaccurate. Stevens arrived at his conclusions as to type of canal after personal examination in the field and study, and not because he found no sea level advocates in the Canal engineering force. This is what President Theodore Roosevelt stated in his February 19, 1906 message to the Congress: ". . . and I call especial attention to the fact that the chief engineer (Stevens) who will be mainly responsible for the success of this mighty engineering feat, and who has therefore a peculiar personal interest in judging aright, is emphatically and earnestly in favor of the lock-canal project and against the sea-level project." In view of this statement by Theodore Roosevelt, the characterization of Stevens as a seeker of unanimity among engineers of the canal construction force is a slur on one of the greatest construction engineers that our country ever produced. For additional information on the contributions of Stevens, see my statement in the *Congressional Record* of May 29, 1956, on "John F. Stevens: Basic Architect of the Panama Canal."

It should be added that Stevens supported the lock type canal in opposition to the majority of the 1905-6 International Board of Consulting Engineers appointed by President Roosevelt to consider the type of canal and had recommended a sea level project. His views were supported by the U.S. Isthmian Canal Commission and Secretary of War, William H. Taft.

Page 13, Paragraph 2

"The administration of Franklin D. Roosevelt clearly changed this stand (of Secretary Hughes) when in 1936 it adjusted the annuity paid to Panama from the original $250,000 to $430,000 to compensate for devaluation of the U.S. dollar; eliminated the U.S. guarantee of Panama's independence; and gave up its right to intervene in Panama's internal affairs."

Comment

In the light of later events and probably more important, the United States in this same treaty (1936) surrendered the 1903 Treaty right to acquire lands and other property within the cities of Panama and Colon and adjacent areas for canal purposes by the "exercise of the right of eminent domain." Had it not been for this right in the 1903 Treaty it is likely that the Canal Zone territory would have been wider than it is.

Page 13, Paragraph 3, Lines 3 to 7

"At the same time (1955), the United States turned over approximately $25 million worth of land together with its improvements including railroad terminals in the cities of Panama and Colon, and, by the same agreement, was relieved of its treaty responsibilities for sanitation in those two cities."

Comment

The 1955 Treaty contemplated the liquidation of the Panama Railroad but the House of Representatives stepped into the situation, and, by an independent investigation, saved the main line of the railroad. Now, there is a railroad without its designed terminal yards and passenger stations. The effort of Panama to collect its own garbage in Panama City and Colon has been a dismal failure and accumulations of garbage in these cities have served as food supply for an increased rat population which has been invading the Canal Zone, and thus has arisen a grave menace to health and sanitation.

In the debate in the Senate during ratification of the 1955 Treaty, the following statement was made by the leading proponent of that treaty: "Since 1936, it has become obvious that Panama is perfectly capable of maintaining adequate sanitary standards in the same cities (Panama and Colon), and in the pending treaty the United States relinquishes that right." The naivete of this view was recognized at the time by informed students of the Canal familiar with the history of Isthmian sanitation.

Page 14, Lines 5 to 8

"The proposal (Terminal Lake-Third Locks Plan) fell into conflict with a renewed interest in the possibility of a sea level canal stimulated by war time development of atomic energy. And in the postwar period, the 'battle of the levels' was reopened."

Comment

This brief paragraph is not an adequate description of this important chapter of canal history. Moreover, it fails to mention the 1947 Report of the Governor of the Panama Canal under Public Law 280, 79th Congress, which under an exaggerated interpretation of the "security" and "national defense" factors in the statute as the controlling considerations, recommended only a Sea Level Project in the Canal Zone. The 1947 report failed to receive Presidential approval and, though transmitted to the

Congress, this body took no action on its recommendations. A comprehensive discussion of the 1947 report will be found in my statement to the House in the *Congressional Record* of June 7, 1962, and on pp. 177-200 of Ho. Doc. No. 474, 89th Congress, under the title of "Isthmian Canal Policy—An Evaluation."

Page 14, Lines 16 to 18

"The *ultimate* solution of the basic problem is probably a sea level canal; but its construction should await a traffic volume that can support the large cost."

Comment

This statement is accurately quoted from par. 15 of Ho. Rept. No. 1960, 86th Congress, but out of context. Significant words in the statement are: (1) "ultimate", which means the most distant; (2) "probably", which indicates uncertainty; and (3) "a", which suggests some other location than the Canal Zone. Omitted in the paragraph is any mention of this report's statements in par. 16 of its doubts "if any reasonable plan to construct a sea-level canal in the Canal Zone could be carried through without serious danger of a long interruption to traffic at the time of cut over from the present lock canal;" also its opinion that "slides of the first magnitude could easily result ... in the short period of unwatering." In addition, this board stressed in par. 13 that "its (sea level canal's) fixed charges are very high, and would commence at the start of the enormous construction job." In the light of the qualifying statements the unqualified advocacy of a sea level project is hardly realistic. It may be added that the above quoted par. 15 is the principal quotation from the 1960 Report used in current sea level propaganda. It conflicts so much with other information in that report that it seems to have been inserted as an after thought. That report with its conflicting statements has the effect of nullifying any firm position.

Page 14, Lines 22 to 24

"... sea level design seems to have won the support of

engineers most closely associated with today's canal operations."

Comment

The engineers referred to are employees carrying out their instructions. In spite of this, some of them have criticized the sea level plan and, as engineers, have privately expressed their preference for the terminal lake proposal as the obvious, economic solution. In addition, experienced, independent engineers, geologists, nuclear physicists, and navigators, including some of the highest eminence, are opposed to the Sea Level Project.

Page 15, First Full Paragraph, Lines 1 to 3

"But Panama has concentrated more on regaining the rights of sovereignty over the Zone than in obtaining ultimate nationalization of the Canal."

Comment

One of the banner signs displayed in radical Panamanian demonstrations was "The Canal Is Ours." It is not possible to separate the question of sovereignty over the Canal Zone and ownership of the Canal any more than it is possible to separate the heart from the body. The conflict between the citizens of Panama and the United States arose because loyal U.S. civilian employees in the Canal Zone understood the dangers and could not be beguiled by official double talk of those temporarily in power in our government who, for reasons best known to themselves, have encouraged Panamanian radicals and attacked our position in the Canal Zone.

Page 15, Last Sentence

". . . Under Secretary of State Livingston T. Merchant was dispatched to Panama in late November (1959) and, while there, reaffirmed, but did not define, Panama's 'titular sovereignty' over the Zone."

Comment

This action taken by Secretary Merchant under instructions,

was a key step in one of the most disgraceful episodes in American history in which the United States allowed itself to be intimidated by Panamanian mobs and was so recognized at the time. I repeatedly tried to have the State Department define "titular sovereignty" but it has steadily refused to do so and by this refusal encouraged further violence. For a discussion of "titular sovereignty—origin and definition," see p. 346 of Ho. Doc. No. 474, 89th Congress, and for an exchange of letters on this subject with the State Department see pp. 387-98 of the same document. The evasions revealed in this exchange are pusillanimous and disgusting.

Page 18, Lines 11 to 14

"The United States also had certain grievances it wished resolved, among them the conveyance of lands next to the U.S. Embassy residence, which had been agreed to in the 1955 treaty."

Comment

In view of the magnitude of the subject under consideration, this is a minor consideration, that hardly deserves mention. Our country in the 1936 and 1955 treaties had given away its bargaining powers and in the September 24, 1965, Presidential announcement, the Executive had indicated its willingness to surrender to major Panamanian demands before the negotiations started. Nor have our negotiators met those demands with equitable counterdemands, such as the extension of the Canal Zone to include the entire watershed of the Chagres River.

Page 19 Last 3 Paragraphs: "Riot of 1964"

"'By the fall of 1963,' Johnson Administration sources have stated, 'we were ready to fly flags together at seventten locations, carefully selected because we realized that this was a very serious and emotional issues. We excluded all schools because we thought that we would have a particularly difficult problem there. We decided that the way to satisfy our obligation to the Panamanians was to fly no flag at all at schools. And this we did. We took down the American flag at Balboa High School during the Christmas vacation in 1963, and when the United States students returned there was no flag flying."[1]

"On the morning of January 7, the students at Balboa High School protested by raising the U. S. flag in front of their school building. Zone authorities took it down. After their first class, students raised it again, and surrounded the flag pole, this time with the support of their parents. The flag, lowered for the night was again raised by the students on January 8 in defiance of a public request from the Zone Governor.

"On January 9, 1964, these students, encouraged by their parents, again defied the Governor's request and again flew the U. S. flag outside the high school. In retaliation, a group of Panamanian students marched into the Zone and tried to raise their flag in front of the school. In the ensuing scuffle the Panamanian flag was torn. The Panamian students then fled from the Zone, destroying property on the way. This was the spark that set off an explosion that had worldwide repercussions. Large crowds formed at the Border of the Zone and serious rioting broke out in Panama City and Colon. The violence continued until January 12, at times becoming a pitched battle between Panamanian citizens and U. S. troops. The Guardia Nacional did not attempt to maintain order. Some 20 Panamanian and four U. S. soldiers were killed in the disturbances. The U. S. troops were not allowed to fire until they had sustained several casualties, whereupon Army marksmen started to return fire from their positions within the Zone against snipers firing into the Zone."

Comment

Much that is confusing has been written about the 1964 flag incident at the Balboa High School but seldom have the following facts been set forth. This was an American High School, on American soil, with normal patriotic American students, who thought they had the right to fly the U. S. flag as is

---

[1] Joseph A. Califano, Jr., at that time Special Assistant to the Secretary and Deputy Secretary of Defense, as quoted in *The Panama Canal*, The Hammarskjold Forms, 1965, p. 51.

done in schools throughout the United States and were infuriated at the supine action of the governing authority of the Zone.

The mob assaults that followed were not caused by the actions of the patriotic students but these were seized upon by radical elements in Panama as an incident to justify what had long been planned in Panama in the way of an attack against the Canal Zone and the treaty rights of the United States. The Panama Government deliberately failed to use its National Guard to maintain order thereby forcing U. S. Armed Forces to defend the lives of our citizens and the Canal.

Instead of being condemned in the press of the United States, these students should have been praised. Were it not for their stand the people of the United States would probably never have learned about what was transpiring concerning the Panama Canal until too late to prevent the planned surrenders at Panama.

In viewing the flag incident it should not be overlooked that it occurred on U. S. territory and not Panamanian. Students from Panama were invaders of the Canal Zone and not the reverse. The mass news media editorial treatment given the Balboa High School students in the United States was in stark contrast to that given many subversive demonstrations in our country and it required many addresses in the Congress by informed members and many articles in periodicals of limited circulation to set the record straight. See my address, "Panama Canal: Focus of Power Politics" and supporting documentation on pp. 305-44 of Ho. Doc. No. 474, 89th Congress, for an extensive discussion of the 1964 mob assault on the Canal Zone.

Page 20, Last Paragraph, First Sentence

"Meanwhile, the National Bar Association of Panama requested the International Commission of Jurists to investigate complaints that the United States had violated the Universal Declaration of Human Rights."

Comment

The facts set forth in the above sentence and the rest of the paragraph are correctly stated but what is not stated is that the Canal Zone is a territorial possession of the United States and that disorders within such territories are domestic concerns of the United States.

Notwithstanding this fact, U. S. authorities cooperated fully with the International Commission of Jurists requested by the National Bar Association of Panama. Its report wholly rejected as baseless the charges by Panama that the United States was the aggressor with respect to the mob assaults and upheld the United States.

Page 21, Lines 5 to 12

"The April 3, (1964) agreement had been interpreted by Panama as an agreement by the United States to negotiate a new treaty to replace that of 1903.... Panama's view is that the present negotiations began on April 3, 1964; but the United States continued to argue against this point until December 18, 1964."

Comment

For clarity and completeness there should be added the following: "at which time the President, upon the recommenda- tion of his advisers, yielded to Panamanian demands as to what the new treaty should provide."

Page 21, Last Paragraph, Lines 1 And 2

"The U.S. Government, meanwhile, undertook an extensive review of its interoceanic canal policy."

Comment

I know of no agency in our government qualified to under- take such review. Since the 1964 riots we have had a plague of amateur canal builders and policy makers who, have been motivated wholly by policies of appeasement and who have completely ignored realistic facts and considerations. The Presi- dent has relied on their findings and recommendations and thus has acquiesced for the surrender of practically all of our indispensable rights as regards the Canal Zone and Canal.

Page 22, Lines 9 to 11

"He (the President) also said that the United States was prepared to negotiate a new treaty with Panama for the existing Canal that would replace the Treaty of 1903."

Comment

This should be qualified by inserting the fact that in so doing the President reversed his earlier position announced on March 16, 1964, before the Organization of American States when he made clear that our Government will always do its best to improve relations with Panama but that under no circumstances will it agree to pre-commitments to renegotiate the 1903 Treaty as the price for resumption of relations with Panama.

Paragraph 22, Last Paragraph

"On September 24, 1965, Johnson and Marco A. Robles, the new president of Panama, issued joint and simultaneous statements in Washington and Panama City on general areas of agreement thus far reached in the three treaties under negotiations. President Johnson's statement included the (5) following points:

"One: The 1903 Treaty will be abrogated.

"Two: The new treaty will effectively recognize Panama's sovereignty over the area of the present Canal Zone.

"Three: The new treaty will terminate after a specific number of years or on the date of the opening of the sea level canal whichever occurs first.

"Four: A primary objective of the new treaty will be to provide for an appropriate political, economic and social integration of the area used in the canal operation with the rest of the Republic of Panama. Both countries recognize there is need for an orderly transition to avoid abrupt and possibly harmful dislocations. We also recognize that certain changes should be made over a period of time. The new canal administration will be empowered to make such changes in accordance with guidelines in the new treaty.

"Five: Both governments recognize the important responsibility they have to be fair and helpful to the employees of all nationalities who are serving so efficiently and well in the operation of the canal. Appropriate arrangements will be made to ensure that the rights and interests of these employees are safeguarded.

"In addition he said:

"'The present canal and any new canal which may be constructed in the future shall be open at all times to the vessels of all nations on a non-discriminatory basis. The tolls would be reasonable in the light of the contribution of the Republic of Panama and the United States of America and of the interest of world commerce.'"

Comment

The joint statement of September 25, 1965, therein quoted meant a complete and abject surrender to Panama of our indispensable sovereignty and authority with respect to the Panama Canal in favor of a dual governmental and managerial setup in an area of endless bloody revolution and political instability. It was obviously the work of inexperienced theorists whose idealism was superior to their judgment.

It is indeed unfortunate that Panamanian policies with respect to these subjects emanate from Red inspired mobs and heedless radicals rather than from objective and realistic Panamanian sources.

Page 23, Last Paragraph, Last Sentence

"The negotiators found it necessary to consult their governments more frequently and in more detail on their respective positions."

Comment

The inference to be derived from this statement is that as the magnitude and complexity of the problems dawned upon the negotiators, their uncertainty and lack of confidence increased.

Page 25, Paragraph 3

"The first treaty proposed concerns abrogating the 1903 treaty, as subsequently adjusted, and its replacement with a new treaty for continued operation and improvements of the existing Canal on terms that are more acceptable to Panama and yet provide for the protection of U. S. investments and interests in the Isthmus and continued efficiency of operation of the Canal at reasonable tolls."

Comments

The continued operation and improvement of the existing canal are authorized by existing treaty under conditions of exclusive responsibility—an obligation assumed under the 1901 Treaty with Great Britain and pursuant to law (Spooner Act of 1902). Experience has shown that this responsibility could not have been met by the United States except with full sovereignty over the Zone. To say the least, it is naive to think that U. S. investments and interest on the Isthmus can be protected and the canal can be efficiently operated with less authority than we now have. This is so because of the inherent situation involved. The Canal Zone cannot be governed satisfactorily by a coalition government and the Canal cannot be operated efficiently under dual management. Moreover, if we go so far as to cede our sovereignty over the Zone to Panama, consent to a dual management these concessions will in nowise mitigate the efforts and demands of Panama that the United States must thereupon surrender all of its authority with respect to the canal enterprise and leave the Isthmus entirely. If the excessive demands of Panama now being acquiesced in by our government can be made effective, then emboldened Panama will soon demand and bring about our complete abandonment of the Canal with resulting chaos. How can our responsible officials assume the role of statesmen when they are so blind, so heedless, and oblivious to what all experience teaches.

Page 25, Last Sentence

"This (Base Rights Agreement) has been the least trouble-some of the three pacts to the two nations . . ."

Comment

This statement is an over simplification and reflects igno-rance. In 1947, despite the approval of a Defense Base Treaty with the United States by the Executive Branch of the Pan-amanian Government, the National Assembly of Panama, after mobs threatened to hang those who should vote for the treaty, unanimously rejected it causing the United States to evacuate a number of bases in Panama that had been maintained by the United States for the protection and defense of both Panama and the Canal, among them the Air Base at Rio Hato. Recent experience in NATO countries shows that Defense Base treaties are only valid at the sufferance of the host country and our government has been derelict and weak in its surrenders at Panama.

Page 28, Lines 8 to 9

". . . hemispheric problems related to extremist subver-sion . . ."

Comment

What is the meaning of the term "extremist subversion?" The only subversion involved is that of the world revolutionary movement known as the international communist conspiracy, for which Castro's Cuba has served as a training ground for waging so-called "wars of national liberation" throughout the Americas, including Isthmian countries. The use of the indicated term has evidently been made to confuse the Panama situation by the use of brave rhetoric to efface the fact that the proposed surrender of our rights at Panama could have the undoubted effect of promoting in that country and other parts of Latin American the self same evils of "extremist subversion" in the Western Hemi-sphere.

Page 29, Lines 6 to 10

"The Panamanians feel the present situation makes them second-class citizens in their own country. The U.S. negotiators wish to accede to Panamanian objectives, but only to the extent that they are compatible with U.S. vital interests of international security and commerce."

Comment

This statement is nonsense, without fact and without foundation. It indicates approval by our brainwashed negotiators of radical and unrealistic Panamanian demands. What are "second class citizens" of Panama? The Canal Zone is not a part of their country but a territorial possession of the United States, with exclusive and indispensable sovereignty granted under treaty and ownership by purchase from individual property owners for the efficient and equitable operation of the Panama Canal.

International security and interoceanic commerce will not be protected by such surrenders and it is not best for Panama that these radical demands become valid. The Panamanian argument might be alright if the Canal enterprise were only commercial; but it is far more than commercial in character. It is one of the great military and transportation keys in the world strategy. As the world at this time is completely out of joint and aggressive revolutionary power is striving to destroy the Free World, it is the quintessence of stupidity for our government to ignore these realistic facts and its solemn responsibility to resist the unreasonable insistence of jingo agitators of Panama. Certainly, the thousands of Panamanians who are employed in the operation of the Canal at higher wages than they ever knew can hardly be called second class citizens.

Page 29, Lines 14 and 15

". . . again raised to $1,930,000 in the Treaty of 1955, which remains the annual payment Panama receives today."

Comment

This statement is incomplete and therefore misleading. There should be added thereto the fact that of the $1,930,000 annuity received by Panama, $1,500,000 is borne by the State Department budget. This separation was brought about by action of the Congress so as not to burden interoceanic commerce by increased tolls. As to the annuity to Panama we can be as liberal as the net income of the canal permits; but any increased annuity would have to be borne in large measure by our already over burdened tax payers or users of the Canal who have to pay tolls. Moreover, if tolls were substantially increased such action would have the undoubted effect of reducing the total shipping using the Canal.

Page 29, Lines 16 to 22

"Panama, fortified by a declaration of the Panamanian Institute of International Law, contends the annuity is not a just and adequate compensation for the use of her greatest natural resource—narrow terrain and geographical position. Panama asserts that this resource is used by the United States to operate a commercial enterprise and for military bases of primary importance to the United States."

Comment

This statement does not mention the more than $100,000,000 that the Panamanian economy receives annually from U. S. sources in the Canal Zone. It is true that the canal enterprise is a business type of activity but, in line with good business methods, it is operated as a self-sustaining basis. As for military bases in Panama, these are important not only to the United States but as well to all of Latin America, including Panama. If it were not for the presence of the United States on the Isthmus, Panama would not and could not exist as a free nation. Moreover, it has a history of centuries of exploitation of travelers at that strategic crossroads that was interrupted at the time of U. S. acquisition of the Canal Zone. Panama must not permit itself to assume the role of a brigand to extort unreasonable revenues from a nation that as long as it is on the Isthmus would fight to the death any attempt to destroy Panamanian Independence.

Whether Panamanian radicals realize or are altogether heedless of this tremendous fact, the citizens of the United States are mindful of it. The people of our country have always held Panama and its people in affectionate esteem but their impatience is mounting because of unreasonable and unrealistic demands stemming largely from communist influence now being voiced by demagogic and self-seeking politicians clothed with brief authority. Such demands, if agreed upon, would surely divest our government of all authority and contact with the canal enterprise and cause the destruction of Panama itself. There are, indeed, none so blind as those who will not see; and in this category may well be included our own negotiators in the present situation.

Page 30, Lines 2 to 5

"... it has been said that the United States considers the present rate of payment too low and would agree to a substantial increase".

Comment

The present annuity to Panama is $1,930,000 of which, as previously stated, $1,500,000 is borne by the State Department budget and $430,000 by canal revenues. The annuity now paid to Panama traces back to the $250,000 annuity paid by the Panama Railroad, which obligation was assumed in the 1903 Treaty. Its increase to $430,000 was a justified adjustment incident to U. S. devaluation of the gold dollar.

The greatest economic benefit to Panama of the presence of the U. S. in the Canal Zone is the more than $100,000,000 from canal sources annually spent in the Republic, and other contributions which results in the highest per capita income in all Latin America. To repeat, any further increase in the annuity would have to be provided either by raising tolls or by the U. S. Taxpayer. Moreover, under the Panama Canal Reorganization Act of 1950 (Public Law 841, 81st Congress), the canal enterprise is required to operate on a self-sustaining basis. Thus, it should be kept entirely separate from any welfare programs for the Republic of Panama.

Page 30, Lines 16 to 18

"But any solution to the revenue question, from the U. S. viewpoint, is dependent upon Panama's acceptance of what the United States considers 'reasonable' tolls."

Comment

The calculation of tolls is necessarily fixed by law enacted by our Congress and Panama has no legal authority to deal with such matters. In this connection, the point should be emphasized tha the Panama Canal does not exist for service as a welfare agency for Panama but for interoceanic commerce of all nations. Why should the Department of State presume to undo by treaty as regards tolls what the Congress, after extensive investigation, established by law?

Page 30, Last Sentence

"The United States is willing to permit the Panamanians to share in responsibility for the management of the existing canal for the rest of its lifetime, but it is basic current U. S. policy to retain final and unimpaired responsibility for the operation and protection of the existing canal."

Comment

This is a direct violation of the Hay-Pauncefote Treaty with Great Britain under which the United States assumed full responsibility for the construction of an Isthmian Canal as well as for the "exclusive right of providing for (its) regulation and management . . ." Also, the 1922 Treaty with Colombia recognized such responsibility as vested "entirely and absolutely" in the United States and not in Panama. The question arises how can the United States have a "current" U. S. Policy that conflicts not only with law but also with important canal treaties with Great Britain and Colombia.

The joint administration of the Panama Canal enterprise with Panama would present an impossible situation of chaotic complexity—management without capitalization and responsibility without authority. As a matter of fact the new treaties now being proposed are altogether in conflict with what has been U. S. policy in that it would dilute and finally destroy the authority of the United States with respect to the Canal.

Page 31, Lines 4 to 10

"In regard to a new canal, the United States proposes a new eleven (11) member canal authority that would give Panama two members until final amortization and three thereafter. The United States would have three members. Three seats would be filled by the nations making the most use of the Canal and three other places would be occupied by representatives of the interests who finance construction. The last would be dropped after amortization, leaving the authority at nine."

Comment

Would a troika of conflicting interests work in managing a great interoceanic canal? Any such body would be a focus of contention with inevitable complications. Moreover, as a back door toward so-called internationalization it would be in clear violation of treaties with Great Britain and Colombia.

Page 33, Lines 15 to 16

"The United States ... in 1955 handed over one of its big hotels to Panama."

Comment

This was the Washington Hotel in Colon. It degenerated in service, finally failed under Panamanian control, and was recently offered for sale. Also, in the 1955 Treaty the United States gave Panama, the two terminal passenger stations and freight yards of the Panama Railroad in Panama City and Colon. Today, they are not used, show the effects of long neglect and Panama no longer receives tax revenues from the Panama Canal Company on those properties.

Page 35, Last Paragraph, Lines 1 to 4

"A number of informed people in both the United States and Panama would agree that settlement of the differences that stem from the 1903 treaty is the first order of business for the negotiators on each side."

Comment

This involves the question of sovereignty in perpetuity and implies a willingness on the part of the U. S. negotiators to surrender our present treaty rights. As to agreeing that such surrenders are the first order of business there are many informed and experienced persons who completely disagree. Nor should it be overlooked that along with the advantages of the geographical location of Panama there are also its perils, for this area of endemic revolution is coveted by predatory powers. As long as the United States is sovereign of the Canal Zone under present treaty provisions, Panama is secure. Thus, in the last analysis, the sovereignty and perpetuity clauses in the 1903 Treaty are best for Panama because it brought about the building of the canal and its operation and maintenance and conferred on Panama independence and great economic betterment. In addition the perpetuity provision precludes the United States from abandoning the existing Canal and this is undoubtedly for the best interests of Panama because it guarantees its perpetual maintenance and operation of the canal by our country. Thus the independence and economic betterment of Panama are perpetually assured. It is, indeed, difficult to understand why this aspect of the situation has never seemed to dawn on Panamanian political leaders.

Page 37, Line 6 From Bottom

". . . how a new canal should be built . . ."

Comment

Under Public Law 88-609, the study group thereby formed was authorized only to determine the feasibility of a sea-level canal. Hence, the quoted expression should read "how a new canal of sea level design should be built." An extensive discussion of the legislative history of the above indicated law can be found on pp. 428-516 of House Document No. 474, 89th Congress, in two of my addresses on the "Interoceanic Canal Problem: Inquiry or Coverup?"

Page 38, Line 5 From Bottom

". . . and a sea-level canal built by conventional means at the present site, and modernization of the present canal."

Comment

This represents the resurrection of the perennial issue of type of canal but the term, "modernization" is not defined, leaving uncertain what is meant. Nor is its consideration authorized under Public Law 88-609.

Page 41, Lines 13 and 14

". . . when and by what means an interoceanic canal should be excavated."

Comment

The type of Canal meant is an "interoceanic canal of sea-level design."

Page 41, Last Paragraph, First Sentence

"The agreement (U. S.-Panama, February 15, 1966, on Route 17) requires the participation of Panamanian officials in the exploration and provision by the United States to Panama of data and conclusions from the surveys."

Comment

There is no provision in Public Law 88-609 authorizing such participation by Panama and the question arises as to what extent is this participation being used to divest the United States of its sovereign rights in the Canal Zone.

Page 47, Lines 9 and 10

"Although it is probable that advance estimates for conventional construction would come close to actual costs . . ."

Comment

The construction of the Panama Canal within the estimates of cost was a source of pride among its builders. More recent experience in the United States, however, shows that the actual cost of large government engineering projects has almost invariably exceeded cost estimates. Thus, the statement is hardly realistic and is misleading.

Page 48, Lines 18 to 21

". . . final decisions will have to be made between 1970 and 1985 whether to build a new canal or merely to improve the existing one, because in either case a ten to fifteen year lead time is needed."

Comment

This obviously refers to the question of building a new canal of sea-level design or the major increase of capacity and operational improvement of the existing high level lake-lock canal. Competent engineers have estimated that the latter would require far less time for construction than the former, far less money; and obviate the necessity for a new treaty.

Page 48, Lines 22 and 23

"As to a sea-level canal, it is assumed that the operating costs would be less than a lock canal."

Comment

This assumption neglects to take into consideration the following:

(a) The large fixed charges for construction.

(b) The huge indemnity required and the greatly increased annuity for the new treaty necessary for a canal at sea-level.

(c) The problem of maintenance which is completely unprecedented in the Isthmian area and which some engineers have warned could be insuperable.

The majority of the panel, evidently relying on data furnished by our responsible authority, utterly ignores the undoubted fact that great slides would attend the deepening of the present or any other cut which would be required by the sea level design. Based on what occurred in the building of the present canal, it is inevitable that any cut for the sea-level project would be attended by slides of first magnitude, thus imposing a vastly increased expenditure over that presented by sea-level advocates.

Page 52, Next To Last Paragraph, Last Sentence

"In addition to the growth in maritime commerce, there is now a trend toward larger ships, as noted earlier, which cannot go through the present canal."

Comment

The present canal, if it had been properly modernized, would be adequate for all commercial vessels except those of the very largest tonnage. As regards the last, there are already supertankers of 250,000 gross tons planned. The economics of super sized vessels is such that they are designed without regard to savings by canal transit and sail around the Cape of Good Hope or through the Straits of Magellan. The Navy long ago eliminated transit of the Panama Canal in ship design because, in war, any type of canal can be destroyed.

Page 57, Last Six Lines

". . . if nuclear excavation is excluded, a sea level canal at any site may be ruled out by economic considerations. The result of this conclusion might be great pressure to expand the present canal facilities by means of new and larger locks, and to augment the water supply by pumping sea water. . . ."

Comment

As to the ruling out of a canal at sea-level, former Canal Zone Governor Jay J. Morrow, a distinguished engineer and man of fine vision, once wrote that "the sea-level project is a hardy perennial, and apparently there will always be someone to argue for it, no matter how often the impossibility of realizing any such scheme within practicable limits of time and cost may be demonstrated." (Ho. Doc. No. 474, 89th Congress, p. 430.)

With regard to the capacity of the present high-level lake-lock canal, former Canal Zone Governor Harry Burgess, a far visioned man and able engineer, made this significant statement: "Considering the low cost of providing water for additional lockages by pumping, it is apparent that the ultimate capacity of the Panama Canal with locks is unlimited, and may be increased to any amount desired by constructing additional locks and installing the necessary pumping equipment." (Ho. Dec. No. 139, 72nd Congress, p. 31.) The cost of such pumping of water into Gatun Lake was estimated at $250.00 per transit, which is inconsequential.

Pages 61 to 63

"Pressures in Panama

"The tendency in some circles is to describe the objectives of Panama as "aspirations" while the objectives of the United States are referred to as "interests." Both nations avowedly have aspirations as well as interests in this or another Panama Canal, but the issue is a more emotional one to Panama. The Panamanians are affected by the day-to-day existence of the Canal much more personally than are most citizens of the United States.

"Panama's team of negotiators and the Robles administration are forced to carry on the discussions with the United States in a domestic political climate that is highly volatile and sensitive to the reactions of its political opponents of all philosophies.

"No Panamanian government could hope to survive a treaty that could be labeled a "sell-out" to the United States. Political opponents of the incumbent administration can be expected to attack any draft treaties that the Robles government reaches agreement upon with the United States. This is one of the reasons why the negotiations have been conducted in secrecy and why even tentative agreements are not disclosed except in the most general way.

"It is of great importance to the status of negotiations that Panama has scheduled national elections in May 1968. Since campaigning for the presidency and other offices begins a full year in advance of the voting in Panama, the Robles government is growing more anxious to reach final settlement with the United States before the campaigning reaches the usual fever heat.

"Robles cannot succeed himself, but his moderate coalition party will face a tough fight from the popular leader of the opposition party, Arnulfo Arias. The Robles coalition has not nominated a candidate, but Arias may be the standard-bearer of the opposition. Robles can be expected to press hard for agreement with the United States before the 1968 voting. How he handles the question of ratification probably is a matter of timing.

"Assuming that most of Panama's aspirations regarding the existing Canal can be satisfied by the United States and tentative agreement is reached by the negotiators before the fall of 1967, Robles probably will call his legislative assembly late in the year, his party probably campaigning on the basis of pacts it can label "triumphs," and obtain ratification after the victory they would expect as an aftermath of the canal agreements.

"Robles' problem is to find a formula with the United States that neither the opposition nor agitators can use as a signal for another outburst of violence in the streets, high schools, and universities.

"To be sure, no agreement between the United States and Panama is going to silence the extreme elements in Panama's body politic. An anti-U. S. plank is traditional in Panamanian political platforms and will probably remain so.

"There are a number of people in the United States who believe that this anti-U. S. sentiment and much of what passes today for nationalism in Panama is part of a long-standing communist plan to wrest control of the Panama Canal, as well as of other strategic waterways of the world, from the hands of the so-called imperialist nations. This plan seems to be aimed at lining up Latin American nations in a bloc in support of Panama against the United States, as was done with the Arab states against England and France in the Suez Crisis of 1956.

"There are others in the United States who feel that a distinction should be made between indigenous nationalism and anti-U. S. harassment aided and abetted by the international communist movement. This group would be inclined to believe that the communist power in Panama lies more in its ability to aggravate a given state of political dissatisfaction than actually to create one, and that the danger there from communism rests on its potential ability to move effectively into a given leadership vacuum, similar to that created in Santo Domingo during the Dominican Republic crisis of 1965.

"Informed sources say that the number of communist organizers in Panama is between fifty and one hundred, and though badly splintered at present, their influence could become wider than this small number would indicate. Some of them recently launched a campaign against U. S. military presence in Panama. The communist efforts are concentrated on the sentiments of ultra-nationalists, and purposely play down the financial and employment benefits that many Panamanians receive from U. S. military operations. These communist efforts could have serious consequences if and when the new base rights and status-of-forces agreement comes up for ratification in the Panamanian Assembly. There is no doubt, however, that the historical tradition of opposition to the United States has contributed much more to the present impasse than anything the communists have done or may do. For example, Panamanian texts used in elementary schools show the United States as an oppressor and even the Catholic bishops jointly signed a declaration[2] which protested U. S. "sovereignty" in the Zone, while deploring the use of force as well as enjoining against communism.

"This combination of local conditions indicates that time is running out for the present Panamanian government, but the United States can take no comfort from an impasse, particularly one that might bring down the Robles government. Robles, it must be remembered, campaigned and won his presidency on a campaign promise to solve the Canal problems with the United States in his term of office. If he does not succeed, the opposition will get a tremendous boost."

Comment

This entire section indicates that the purposes of the negotiations are to prevent the overthrow of the present Administration in Panama, to bring about its victory in 1968, and to placate Panamanian mobs. The Panama Canal certainly should not be used as a pawn in Panamanian politics and it would not have become one if our responsible officials, especially those in the State Department, had asserted our just rights with requisite frankness. This section is really a description of one of the most deplorable situations in United States diplomatic history. Nothing could be more futile than to try to adjust U. S. canal policy to the vagaries of Panamanian volatility, to satiate the insatiable, or to deal with the canal enterprise as a purely welfare agency of the Panamanian Government.

Pages 63 to 65

"Disposition of Congress"

"Panama has its Assembly, and the United States has its Congress. Both legislative bodies will be called upon to approve new treaties, which may be agreed upon by the negotiators. Consequently, each negotiating team must be keenly aware of the other's legislative frame of reference.

---

[2] Dr. Isais Batista Ballesteros, *El Drama de Panama y América,* Panamá, 1965, p. 310.

"The U.S. Congress maintains close surveillance over U.S.-Panamanian relations through committee responsibilities for foreign affairs, for the merchant marine, for the armed services, for commerce, and for appropriations. All these involve U.S. activities dealing with the Canal, its operation and defense. Through briefing furnished from time to time by U.S. officials, appropriate committees of Congress are kept in touch with significant developments on Canal matters.

"Congressional sentiment on the basic objective of U.S. policy is clear: the United States must continue to defend the Canal and maintain it as an efficient crossroads for marine commerce. This is regarded not as a matter of U.S.-Panamanian policy alone, but as one affecting the inter-American defense and communications systems. Since it is generally agreed that the present lock Canal will eventually become inadequate, it is recognized that either the present Canal will have to be modernized or that a new canal will have to be constructed in its stead. The Congress is not convinced that the major responsibilities of implementing either plan could be carried out by Panama. Here, the aspiration of Panama is considered to far exceed the realities.

"There is some cleavage in U.S. Congressional opinion on how the basic U.S. objectives can best be attained in connection with the Panama Canal. The present administration in the United States did clear the terms stated in the three draft treaties handed to Panama with some key members of Congress in earlier stages of the negotiations. The party structure in Congress, however, underwent significant changes in November, 1966, and there has been a rise in guns-or-butter sentiment in Washington that already has been felt in economy measures.

"Also there is a group on Capitol Hill, which has support from at least two national veterans organizations, that sees no need for a sea-level canal and warns against the concessions to Panama that would be involved in the three treaties. This group cannot be disregarded; its influence may be enhanced by the recent changes in composition of the U.S. Congress. Despite the fact that the negotiators and their respective governments favor a sea-level canal, this group feels the only reasonable and economic course is to improve the lock-lake design of the present facility. Though this alternative plays little part in the current negotiations between Panama and the United States, it is being given consideration by the study groups concerned with the economic aspects of alternatives to the present Canal.

"In sum, a set of treaties that might have easily passed through the Senate to ratification a year ago might well face heavier going if submitted today. It is also significant that, although there is articulate opposition in the Senate and House to scrapping the 1903 treaty with Panama, this is not balanced by legislators who feel as strongly the other way. The majority leadership of Congress, however, could probably be persuaded as to the need for a sea-level canal and would be prepared to make certain concessions on some of the irritating points of difference between the United States and Panama. These concessions could concern some form of sovereignty, wage scales, terms of employment, joint operation of the Canal and increased U.S. payments. But they would not include yielding prime U.S. rights and responsibility for operation and defense of the Canal complex."

Comment

This section undertakes to summarize the attitude of the Congress as regards the proposed treaties, which it states were cleared with key members of the Congress. The treaties were not cleared with some of the best informed leaders in the Congress on the canal question, who were altogether ignored.

The section states also that the majority leadership would probably make concessions to Panama on sovereignty but would not yield prime U.S. rights and responsibility for operation and defense. In the very nature of the situation, this statement is self-contradictory for where there is responsibility there must be authority of adequate character. No enterprise such as the Panama Canal can function under a dual management and control and many members of the Congress recognize the truth of this fact as the result of various ill-fated attempts to establish coalition governments following World War II. It must be said now, as it was said of old, that one cannot serve two master.

Page 64, Lines 3 to 6

"The U. S. Congress maintains close surveillance over U. S.-Panamanian relations through committees responsible for foreign affairs, for the merchant marine, for the armed services, for commerce, and for appropriations."

Comment

Though administrative officials have briefed various committees, they all speak with one voice reflecting so-called official views usually prepared to support pre-determined objectives. In this way, the Congress has been denied information of vital importance that often vitiates the views presented.

Page 65, Next To Last Paragraph

"Some Panamanian and U. S. officials have shown signs of uneasiness at the slow pace of the negotiations. . . . Both nations well recall the riots of January 1964 and appear to believe the same thing could happen again if the negotiations are not successfully concluded before the Panamanian election campaign gets into high gear."

Comment

The reasons for the 1964 riots were the failure of our high officials during recent years to clarify and make definite U. S. canal policies and the naive effort to stop minor violence with a succession of surrenders, all of which, as was foreseen and predicted, culminated in the January 1964 mob assault on the Canal Zone.

As to whether completing the negotiations before the Panamanian election campaign starts will avoid violence, a leading opposition candidate for the Presidency of Panama has publicly warned that no treaty negotiated by the present administration will be approved by the People of Panama. To emphasize that possibility, we have the example of the rejection in 1947 of the Defense Base Treaty. On that occasion, the mob surrounded the Capitol of Panama, and threatened to hang all members of the

Assembly who approved the treaty; and in fear they voted unanimously its rejection amid scenes of unbelievable terror.

Page 65, Lines 4 to 5 From Bottom

"'If this thing isn't settled fairly soon we may all be hanging from lamp posts,' says one Panamanian official."

Comment

This is no place to quote such an alarmist statement, for the only purpose served is to create fear as the basis for diplomatic action. We are asked to share authority over the Canal with this type of mob-dominated Panamanian leadership. If we had continued our policy of just, wise and realistic motivation, mob violence could not have entered the picture.

Page 66, Lines 1 to 3

"Violence, once turned on by whatever source, would be difficult to limit and the mobs are as likely to seek out Panamanian leaders as they are to seek targets in the Canal Zone."

Comment

Informed persons have long recognized that the Panama route is the best site for a canal and look upon other sites in Panama as political diversions. Moreover, the present canal has enormous facilities constructed over many decades, excellent port facilities, protected anchorages, and a sanitary policy that has been eminently successful. A plan that proposes to abandon such investments and advantages in cavalier manner is highly extravagant, utterly unrealistic, and criminally stupid.

Page 66, Lines 16 to 20

"They (U.S. and Panamanian officials) are aware that the United States has not yet solved the problems of the technology of nuclear excavation and has no agreement with other signatories of the Limited Nuclear Test Ban Treaty that would permit atomic excavation even if it were certified as technically feasible."

Comment

In addition, there are distinguished nuclear physicists who view such excavation as "insanity." Certainly, before attempting so vast a project as an interoceanic canal there ought to be some experience elsewhere. In any event, a change in the Test Ban Treaty would be difficult, if not altogether impossible to obtain.

Page 66, Third Paragraph From Bottom

"The United States Government knows full well that all the nations of Latin America are watching closely to see what kind of treatment is accorded Panama in the current treaty negotiations."

Comment

The Panamanian Government has carried on a systematic campaign of arousing the support of other Latin countries but, so far as known, the Government of the United States has not met this campaign with forthright public statements but, by its silence, has encouraged such efforts.

In the case of Colombia, the sovereign of the Isthmus before the independence of Panama, that country has been collecting documents on the Panama Canal in the United States over a period of years. This is most significant.

Page 67, Last Paragraph

"The Government of the Republic of Panama will continue to promote the extension to other countries of the Central American Isthmus of the indirect benefits of . . . a new Panama Canal Treaty. . . . This objective is pursued . . . as evidence of a regional feeling . . ., etc."

Comment

This quotation is a vague statement by the Foreign Minister of Panama, suggesting that Panama wishes to extend benefits of the Canal to the entire Central American Isthmus, and in utter disregard of the costs to users of the canal in way of tolls and the American taxpayer. As it is nothing but bombast, this quotation does not merit repeating in any worthwhile study. The canal should be, and must be, operated to serve all the world and not only a part of it.

Pages 88 and 89

"A. The Choco Development Project"

Comment

This section of the appendix contains useful information about the Choco Project but does not evaluate it from the marine operational standpoint. In a statement to the House on February 1, 1967, I commented at length on its navigational features emphasizing how the plan for its construction is an application of the lake-lock principle used in the construction of the Panama Canal.

What was the outcome of this historic address? It mobilized the Congress. The danger of the proposed treaties was dramatized. We quote from the Allen-Goldsmith Report in *Human Events:*

"These treaties evoked such a storm of disapproval in Congress that they were never signed. Some 150 House members sponsored denunciatory resolutions. They made three charges: That the agreements ceded sovereignty over the canal to Panama; made that country a 'partner' in canal management, and would share its defense with Panama; authorized the U.S. to construct a new canal in Panama.

"The uproar over these treaties were so massive and vehement that the Johnson Administration shelved them. No effort has ever been made to revive them."

The elected representatives of the people of the United States had rallied around the words of Congressman Flood. The treaties were not ratified. Loss of United States sovereignty over the Panama Canal Zone was narrowly averted. Our nation passed a major crisis with ramifications which could have borne untold cost for future generations.

On December 6, 1971, fighting West Point graduate Congressman John M. Murphy from New York City (Democrat), Chairman of the Panama Canal Subcommittee of the Merchant Marine and Fisheries Committee of the House of Representatives, who later valiantly risked the ire of the Communists, the Mafia, the Panamanian Government and the U. S. State Department in order to destroy the narcotics traffic flowing through Panama, reiterated the stand of Congressman Flood's historic address. Congressman Murphy said: "I assert here this morning that *no treaty* involving an appropriation of monies or a release of property belonging to the United States can be concluded unless proper recognition is granted to the jurisdiction of the House. I have a duty to this Congress to uphold its authority and I fully intend to do so. This duty transcends any treaty with Panama, and goes to the very core of the purpose and power of the House of Representatives."

So today, as in 1967, Congressman Flood has staunch allies in the House of Representatives in the fight against those who would give away U. S. interests in the Panama Canal.

Chapter Seven

U.S.-Panamanian Relations

In its relations with Panama the United States has met its treaty obligations as regards the Panama Canal and has always been conscious of the just needs of Panama. For example, a significant defect in the Hay-Bunau-Varilla Treaty was its failure to provide an adequate crossing of the Canal for use after its opening to traffic.

To correct the situation in which Panama had been cut in two by the Canal, the Congress in 1930 authorized the establishment of a toll free passenger and vehicular ferry system at Balboa and highway in the Canal Zone on the west bank of the Canal connecting the ferry with the highways of Panama, both officially named in honor of the former Governor of the Canal Zone and Congressman from Kentucky, Maurice H. Thatcher, who was the author of the legislation. The ferry was replaced in 1962 by the Thatcher Ferry Bridge, also officially named by the Congress in his honor.

The United States has always taken into consideration the economic and sociological elements connected with its sovereignty over the Canal Zone. It eliminated the danger to Panama's internal affairs which might have arisen from private Panamanian or U.S. ownership of land in the Canal Zone for, in addition to obtaining the grant by Panama of the attributes of sovereignty en bloc, the United States obtained ownership of all privately owned land and property in the Canal Zone by purchase from individual owners, making the Zone our most costly territorial acquisition.

Despite the best efforts of the United States to encourage stability and progress in Panama, the history of that small nation has been marked by many episodes of near anarchy and a stifling of progress by its oligarchy. On August 7, 1969 Congressman Flood addressed the House of Representatives on the problems Panamanian history would forecast if we were to abdicate our responsibilities for operating and maintaining the Panama Canal:

PANAMA: LAND OF ENDEMIC REVOLUTION REQUIRES OBJECTIVE EVALUATION.

In various addresses in and out of the Congress, I have repeatedly described the Isthmus of Panama as a land of endemic revolution and endless political turmoil. In contrast, the constitutionally acquired domain of the United States known as the Canal Zone has been an "island" of stability and security. To that territory, on many occasions, Panamanian leaders have fled for a haven of refuge to escape assassination.

The latest example of such use by Panamanian leaders was on October 11, 1968, when the duly elected President of Panama, Dr. Arnulfo Arias, with high officials of his government, after having served only 11 days, was overthrown in a military coup d'etat and sought a sanctuary in the zone territory.

Some years prior to this, and following a series of incidents, which included invasions of the Canal Zone by Panamanian mobs that required the use of U.S. Armed Forces to protect the lives of our citizens and to prevent injury to the Panama Canal, the basis was laid for surrender to Panama by the United States of its ownership and control of what is the jugular vein of the Americas.

This development, aided and abetted by elements in the Department of State for more than a decade of its Panama Canal policy control, culminated in the announcement on June 26, 1967, by the Presidents of the United States and Panama of completion of negotiations for three proposed new canal treaties. Fortunately for the United States and all countries that use the Panama Canal, through the journalistic initiative of the Chicago Tribune, the texts of these treaties were obtained at Panama and published in the United States. They produced strong opposition in our country, Panama and important maritime nations that use the canal, and were never signed.

Briefly stated, these proposed treaties provided for first, ceding to Panama of sovereignty over the Canal Zone and making that country a partner in canal management; second, sharing the defense of the canal with Panama; and, third, authorizing the United States to construct a new canal in Panama. These treaty proposals would ultimately give to that country not only the existing canal, but also any new canal in Panama that the United States might construct to replace it. Moreover, the negotiators of these treaties ignored article IV, section 3, clause 2 of the U.S. Constitution, which specifically vests the power to dispose of territory and other property of the United States in the Congress and not in the treaty-making agency of our Government consisting of the President and the Senate. This action by the treaty negotiators was in line with my repeated predictions that elements in the Department of State would attempt to accomplish by treaty what could never be put over by statute.

As a consequence of the preparation of these treaties, some 150 Members of the House introduced or cosponsored resolutions opposing any cession of U.S. authority over the Canal Zone or Panama Canal, and the House Committee on Foreign Affairs held extensive hearings. Unfortunately, these hearings were never published and they certainly should be.

In recent weeks, the Spanish language press of Panama has reported with increasing frequency that the present Government of Panama hopes to reopen negotiations for new canal treaties. This information, coupled with reports of consideration of an official of our Foreign Service, associated with the formulation of the discredited 1967 canal treaties, for appointment as U.S. Ambassador to Panama, represents an ominous situation to which the Congress should not appoint as Ambassador to Panama any participant in the abortive 1967 giveaway treaties, but someone who will defend the indispensable sovereign rights, power and authority of the United States.

The location of the Panama Canal at the crossroads of the Americas is a perilous one. As the canal has been a prime target of Soviet policy since 1917 in the struggle for world domination, the people of our country, do not realize the danger involved. Because of that, I shall elaborate.

The record of political upheavals and sanguinary strife on the Isthmus of Panama antedates the Panama Revolution of 1903 by many years. When the United States, under, the dynamic leadership of President Theodore Roosevelt, undertook the great task of constructing an Isthmian Canal at Panama, they studied the subject in all its essential features. They well knew that unless complete and absolute stability in political and governmental conditions was permanently maintained in the Canal Zone, it would be useless for the United States to assume its 1901 treaty obligation with Great Britain — Hay-Pauncefote Treaty — to construct and operate the proposed interoceanic waterway. This fact, Mr. Speaker, was also clearly understood by Panamanian leaders of the 1903 movement for secession from Colombia and by officials of the Panama Government following independence.

Because of their knowledge of isthmian history and appreciation of the necessity for maintaining free and uninterrupted transit, the treaty making authorities of both the United States and Panama undertook to provide in the basic canal treaty of November 18, 1903, clearcut and unconditional provisions granting complete and exclusive sovereignty over the Canal Zone to the United States in perpetuity. The United States could not afford to undertake the great enterprise except under the conditions of such control, and Panama itself could not afford to do less than the grant of full control of both the zone territory and the canal itself to the United States.

With such stability thus guaranteed, the United States

undertook the execution of the canal project and its subsequent maintenance, operation, sanitation, and protection. The net investment of the American taxpayers in it from 1904 to June 30, 1968, including defense, totals more than $5 billion.

Striking evidence of the recognition by President Theodore Roosevelt as to the transcendent importance for political stability in the Canal Zone is to be noted in his December 7, 1903, annual message to the Congress, a short time after Panamanian independence.

Commenting on the Panama Revolution of 1903 and the conduct of the United States in connection therewith, President Roosevelt supplied the Congress with valuable information, which I insert at this point:

When these events happened, 57 years had elapsed since the United States had entered into its treaty with New Granada. During that time the Governments of New Granada and of its successor, Colombia, have been in a constant state of flux. The following is a partial list of the disturbances on the Isthmus of Panama during the period in question as reported to us by our consuls. It is not possible to give a complete list, and some of the reports that speak of revolutions must mean unsuccessful revolutions:

May 22, 1850: Outbreak; two Americans killed; war vessel demanded to quell outbreak.

October 1850: Revolutionary plot to bring about independence of the isthmus.

July 22, 1851: Revolution in four southern provinces.

November 14, 1851: Outbreak at Chagres. Man-of-war requested for Chagres.

June 2, 1853: Insurrection at Bogotá, and consequent disturbance on isthmus. War vessel demanded.

May 23, 1854: Political disturbances; war vessel requested.

June 28, 1854: Attempted revolution.

October 24, 1854: Independence of isthmus demanded by provincial legislation.

April 1856: Riot, and massacre of Americans.

May 4, 1856: Riot.

May 18, 1856: Riot.

October 2, 1856: Conflict between two native parties. United States forces landed.

December 18, 1858: Attempted secession of Panama.

April 1859: Riots.

September 1860: Outbreak.

October 4, 1860: Landing of United States forces in consequence.

May 23, 1861: Intervention of the United States forces required by Intendente.

October 2, 1861: Insurrection and civil war.

April 4, 1862: Measures to prevent rebels crossing isthmus.

June 13, 1862: Mosquera's troops refused admittance to Panama.

March 1865: Revolution and United States troops landed.

August 1865: Riots; unsuccessful attempt to invade Panama.

March 1866: Unsuccessful revolution.

April 1867: Attempt to overthrow the government.

August 1867: Attempt at revolution.

July 5, 1868 — Revolution; provisional government inaugurated.

August 29, 1863: Revolution; provisional government overthrown.

April 1871: Revolution; followed apparently by counter-revolution.

April 1873: Revolution and civil war which lasted to October 1875.

August 1876: Civil war which lasted until April 1877.

July 1878: Rebellion.

December 1878: Revolt.

April 1879: Revolution.

June 1879: Revolution.

March 1883: Riot.

May 1883: Riot.

June 1884: Revolutionary attempt.

December 1884: Revolutionary attempt.

January 1885: Revolutionary disturbances.

March 1885: Revolution.

April 1887: Disturbances on Panama Railroad.

November 1887: Disturbance on line of canal.

January 1889: Riot.

January 1895: Revolution which lasted until April.

March 1895: Incendiary attempt.

October 1899: Revolution.

February to July 1900: Revolution.

January 1901: Revolution.

July 1901: Revolutionary disturbances.

September 1901: City of Colon taken by rebels.

March 1902: Revolutionary disturbances.

July 1902: Revolution.

The above is only a partial list of the revolutions, rebellions, insurrections, riots, and other outbreaks that have occurred during the period in question; yet they number 53 for the 57 years. It will be noted that 1 of them lasted for nearly 3 years before it was quelled; another for nearly a year. In short, the experience of over half a century has shown Colombia to be utterly incapable of keeping order on the isthmus. Only the active interference of the United States has enabled her to preserve so much as a semblance of sovereignty. Had it not been for the exercise by the United States of the police power in her interest, her connection with the isthmus would have been sundered long ago. In 1856, in 1860, in 1873, in 1885, in 1901, and again in 1902, sailors and marines from United States warships were forced to land in order to patrol the isthmus, to protect life and property and to see that the transit across the isthmus was kept open. In 1861, in 1862, in 1885, and in 1900 the Colombian Government asked that the United States Government would land troops to protect its interests and maintain order on the isthmus.

Mr. Speaker, at the time of the 1903 Panama Revolution, President Roosevelt acted under the authority of the treaty of 1846 between the United States and New Granada — now Colombia — guaranteeing the neutrality of the isthmus to the end that free transit would not be interrupted or embarrassed. The result of his denial of transit over the Panama Railroad by either Panamanian revolutionists or the Colombian Army was that the 1903 revolution was bloodless and the provisions of the 1846 treaty were upheld.

What has been the record of civil strife and political turmoil in the Republic of Panama since the establishment of Panamanian independence and U.S. occupation in 1904 of the Canal Zone? The following highlights, gleaned from authoritative sources, though not complete, are most revealing:

November 14, 1904: Seditious and mutinous conduct of the army of Panama (now National Police), with discovery of a plot to arrest President Amador, which was averted by diplomatic representations of the United States to preserve constitutional order as provided by treaty and the constitution of Panama.

October 11, 1925: Riot in Panama City with 1 person killed and 11 wounded, requiring assistance by United States Army to quell.

January 2, 1931: Revolution in Panama, requiring intervention of the United States Minister to save lives of Panamanian officials and the President, who were held prisoners, and resulting in the enforced resignation of the President.

November 22, 1940: National Assembly adopted new constitution proposed by President Arnulfo Arias.

October 9, 1941: Bloodless revolution ousted President Arias and installed Ricardo Adolfo de la Guardia as Provisional President.

Late 1944: Suspension of constitution caused 14 Panamanian Assemblymen (Congressmen) to flee to the Canal Zone.

June 15, 1945: Constituent Assembly met, received resignation under duress of de la Guardia as Provisional President, and elected Enrique A. Jiminez as his successor.

December 1, 1945: Armed revolt, for which former President Arnulfo Arias was thrown into prison charged with participation, but was acquitted on July 29, 1946.

March 1, 1946: Constituent Assembly approved new constitution replacing the totalitarian instrument of former President Arnulfo Arias.

December 22, 1947: In the midst of disorder, National

Assembly unanimously rejected a defense base treaty with the United States.

February 1948: United States announced withdrawal of all troops from military bases in the Republic, as a consequence of the indicated rejection, and at considerable financial loss.

July 28, 1949: First Vice President Daniel Chanis, Jr., succeeded ailing President Domingo Diaz Arosemena, on latter's resignation.

November 18, 1949: President Chanis accused Col. Jose Remon, Chief of Police, of operating illegal monopolies, and dismissed him.

November 20, 1949: President Chanis was forced to resign under pressure of national police headed by Colonel Remon, and Vice President Roberto F. Chiari was sworn in as President.

November 22, 1949: National Assembly voted for reinstatement of Chanis as President.

November 24, 1949: Supreme Court upheld the claim of Chanis but, with support of National Police, former President Arnulfo Arias again became President on the contention of his sponsors that at the preceding election he had in fact defeated his opponent, Diaz, whose election had been officially declared, followed by his assumption of the Presidency.

November 25, 1949: United States suspended relations with Panama because of overthrow of "constituted authorities."

November 26, 1949: Chanis and two other former Presidents fled to the Canal Zone to escape arrest.

December 14, 1949: United States recognized the Arnulfo Arias regime.

May 7, 1951: President Arnulfo Arias decreed suspension of the constitution and dissolution of the National Assembly.

May 10, 1951: After bitter street fighting President Arias surrendered to Colonel Remon, Chief of National Police. Impeachment by the National Assembly of President Arias and naming of First Vice President Alcibiades Arosemena as constitutional President resulted, and was upheld by the Supreme Court.

October 1, 1951: Jose Remon inaugurated as President.

January 2, 1955: President Remon assassinated.

January 3, 1955: First Vice President Jose Ramon Guizado sworn in as President.

January 15, 1955: President Ramon Guizado removed from office and placed under arrest, charged with being implicated in the President Remon assassination, impeached, found guilty, and sentenced by the National Assembly to 10 years' imprisonment, of which sentence he served a portion but was later released.

May 2, 1958: Panamanian University students planted 72 Panamanian flags at various locations in Canal Zone, including one in front of the Canal administration building, without any authority therefor.

May 5, 1958: University students marched on presidential palace in Panama City, demanding immediate steps in behalf of Panamanian sovereignty over Canal Zone.

May 20, 1958: Six days of street fighting and bloodshed in Panama City and Colon, requiring use of the Panamanian National Guard to restore order.

December 18, 1958: Panamanian enactment declaring the extension of Panama's territorial waters from the three mile limit to a twelve mile limit, encircling the Canal Zone which led to a U.S. protest.

January 13, 1959: Panama National Assembly, after receipt of U.S. protest, voted not to reconsider its action.

November 3, 1959: Panamanian mobs invaded the Canal Zone, overwhelming civilian police, requiring the use of the U.S. Army to protect the lives of our citizens and the Canal.

November 28, 1959: Panamanian mobs attempted to invade the Zone but were repelled by the U.S. Army until it was relieved by the Panamanian National Guard, which latter force restored order.

September 17, 1960: President Eisenhower, in a mistaken gesture of friendship, authorized the display of one Panamanian flag in the Canal Zone at Shaler's Triangle as evidence of Panama's so-called "titular sovereignty" over the Zone Territory.

October 12, 1962: Ceremonies for the dedication of the

Thatcher Ferry Bridge disrupted by Panamanian demonstrations.

October 29, 1962: Panamanian flag officially raised at the Canal Zone Administration Building on authorization of President Kennedy, as part of a program for displaying it at other locations in the Zone.

March, 1963: President Chiari of Panama at the San José Conference with President Kennedy raised the threat of "radical action".

January 9—12, 1964: Panamanian mobs attacked the Canal Zone requiring the use of the U.S. Army to protect the lives of our citizens and to prevent injury to the Canal during which attack the Panamanian National Guard, on orders of the President of Panama, remained in their barracks and did nothing whatsoever to quell the mob, which, unrestrained, also looted and burned American owned property in the City of Panama. Several U.S. soldiers were killed.

October 11, 1968: Military coup d'etat overthrowing the legally elected government and establishing a revolutionary provisional government of Panama.

Mr. Speaker, at this point it is well to stress that the 1903 treaty granted to the United States the right and authority to enforce sanitary measures of preventive or curative character in the cities of Panama and Colon; also the same right and authority to maintain public order in the event of the inability of Panama to perform this duty.

In the 1936 treaty, the authority of the United States to maintain order in the terminal cities was abrogated. In the 1955 treaty, the right of the United States to enforce sanitary ordinances in the terminal cities was likewise revoked as was also the power of eminent domain in the Republic of Panama for canal purposes, all these at the insistence of Panama. Together, those actions definitely weakened the United States in meeting its responsibilities for the maintenance, operation, sanitation, and protection of the Panama Canal. Their effect was the withdrawal of U.S. activities to the limits of the Canal Zone Territory.

When the above enumerated records of violence on the isthmus are viewed, with the perspective now possible, it is obvious that conditions on the isthmus have changed since 1904, but they have changed for the worse. Instead of the United States permitting its rights, power, and authority to be eroded further they should be strengthened in the direction of the original grants of the 1903 treaty with extension of the Canal Zone to include the entire watershed of the Chagres River.

In summation, Mr. Speaker, I would stress the following:

First. Panama is still a land of endemic revolution and political turmoil.

Second. U.S. surrender of its full sovereign powers is not realistic, but fraught with the gravest peril for the security of the Americas.

Third. We should have at Panama as our Ambassador one who will defend the rights, powers, and authority of the United States and not one who would acquiesce in their surrender or subversion.

Fourth. We should remove the Department of State from control of U.S. Panama Canal policy.

Mr. Speaker, nothing that I have ever said in my discussions on the Panama Canal was intended to be evidence of any unkindness toward Panama and its people, but only an objective and realistic presentation of facts. Unfortunately, Panama has been, and is, a most fruitful soil of bloody riots and revolutions and such conditions cannot be ignored or swept under the rug in any evaluation of the Panama Canal enterprise. Demagogic intentions have no place in the equation. The questions involved must be dealt with on the highest and most realistic plane of statesmanship. Theodore Roosevelt, in his message to the Congress previously quoted, had no motive of malice whatsoever and was simply stating facts of history that had to be considered by our Government in the formulation of our canal policy. In this connection, I would urge that the formulation of current canal policy should be taken away from the Department of State unless that department is completely revolutionized and realistic, capable officials are substituted for the weak, and vascillating un-Americans supplanted.

Another vital point in these discussions which must be taken into account is the manifest policy of Soviet power to take over all the strategic waterways of the world and thus obtain the strangleholds on the world. Not only has Soviet policy been addressed toward the liquidation of U.S. authority over the Panama Canal but every move under that policy has been made for the purpose of capturing all such strategic maritime routes to enlarge Soviet power. Thus the Suez Canal has come under Soviet domination and is now indefinitly closed to traffic, a situation that is far more serious to the free world than to Soviet nations.

Finally, in common with all of our citizens, I hope to see the people of Panama ruled by officials chosen by them in free and fair elections and the maintenance of a stable government under which the country can develop its large potential and become an outstanding example of domestic tranquillity and progress. As evidence of my interest in Panama, I have introduced a bill for the major modernization of the Panama Canal. This measure, which was quoted in a statement in the Congress by me on February 19, 1969, not only provides for the best solution of the interoceanic canal problem, but also protects the economic well-being of the people of Panama.

*   *   *

The Thurmond-Flood bills for major modernization of the Panama Canal were designed with full consideration given to the impact of the work to be undertaken on the Republic of Panama.

With a policy of noninterference in the internal affairs of our neighbors we can do no more. But ethically, as a great power with a territorial possession geographically of such great importance to the economy of a small nation, we can do no less.

Too often in the past we have undertaken programs of great magnitude which have dislocated local economies and thus have caused so much harm that we have cancelled out the benefits derived from the program! In a case involving a large capital expenditure, such as that entailed by the Thurmond-Flood bills, in which the effect on a small country will be great, it is to our credit as a nation that we have not ignored the economic consequences our expenditures will have. I can only wish that as much attention had been paid to the dangers of the spiral of creeping inflation which we now face in our domestic affairs.

Latin America is now faced by the danger of radical, Communist dominated revolutions influenced by the "attractions" of Fidelismo. That Castro has in fact failed in Cuba is immaterial to these revolutionaries. Their attention is only focused upon the internal situation in their own countries.

The problems of Latin America cannot be solved by perpetuation of the status quo. They cannot be solved by radical surgery either. I do not presume to know what should be done by the United States in relation to Latin America, other than that we should pay more attention to our neighbors, their psychology and their quest for *dignitad*.

I do know that the major modernization of the Panama Canal espoused by the Thurmond-Flood bills is an indispensable step in the right direction. I do know that men of good will exercising honesty in their relationships can accomplish wonders.

That we should now implement the needed improvements in the Panama Canal will, minimally, show our neighbors that our efforts are not merely lip service toward hemispheric solidarity. Maximally, it may act as a catalyst for a true Alliance for Progress.

Chapter Eight

A Call to Action

On September 5, 1969 the Panamanian press reported that the United States Department of State will accept any initiative from Panama to resume conversations on Canal Zone Treaty negotiations. The Panamanian government promptly appointed negotiators.

These events raised a hue and cry in the Congress of the United States. Identical House of Representatives Resolutions, initiated by Congressman Flood (Dem. Pa.), Congresswoman Leonor K. Sullivan (Dem. Mo.), Congressman Durward G. Hall (Rep. Mo.), and Congressman Samuel L. Devine (Rep. Ohio), has been sponsored by more than 100 Members of Congress.

The text of this Resolution is as follows:

RESOLUTION

Whereas it is the policy of the House of Representatives and the desire of the people of the United States that the United States maintain its sovereignty and jurisdiction over the Panama Canal Zone; and

Whereas under the Hay-Pauncefote Treaty of 1901 between Great Britain and the United States, the United States adopted the principles of the Convention of Constantinople of 1888 as the rules for the operation, regulation, and management of said canal; and

Whereas by the terms of the Hay-Bunau-Varilla Treaty of 1903, between the Republic of Panama and the United States, under the authority of the perpetuity of use, occupation, control construction, maintenance, operation, sanitation and protection for said canal was granted to the United States; and

Whereas the United States has paid the Republic of Panama almost $50,000,000 in the form of a gratuity; and

Whereas the United States has made an aggregate investment in said canal in an amount of over $5,000,000,000; and

Whereas said investment or any part thereof could never be recovered in the event of Panamanian seizure or United States abandonment; and

Whereas under Article IV, Section 3, Clause 2 of the United States Constitution, the power to dispose of territory or other property of the United States is specifically vested in the Congress; and

Whereas 70 per centum of the Canal Zone traffic either originates or terminates in United States ports; and

Whereas said canal is of vital strategic importance and imperative to the hemispheric defense and to the security of the United States; and

Whereas, during the preceding administration, the United States conducted negotiations with the Republic of Panama which resulted in a proposed treaty under the terms of which the United States would shortly relinquish its control over the Canal; and

Whereas there is reason to believe that the present dictatorship in control of the Government of Panama seeks to renew negotiations with the United States looking toward a similar treaty; and

Whereas the present study being conducted by the Atlantic-Pacific Interoceanic Canal Study Commission may result in a decision to utilize the present canal as a part of a new sea level canal; and

Whereas any action looking toward an agreement with the Government of Panama which would affect the interest of the United States in the Canal would be premature prior to the submission of the report of the Commission in any event;

> *Resolved* by the House of Representatives, that it is the sense of the House of Representatives that the Government of the United States maintain and protect its sovereign rights and jurisdiction over said canal and that the United States Government in no way forfeit, cede, negotiate, or transfer any of these sovereign rights or jurisdiction to any other sovereign nation or to any international organization.

This type of move by the Department of State — unwarranted, untimely and potentially detrimental to our national interests — has been too typical throughout successive administrations. This is not to say that the Department of State has not produced many able diplomats and statesmen, Ambassador Robert Murphy and Ambassador Loy Henderson, among others. The State Department has also had outstanding Panama Canal experts associated with it from time to time, such as William Franklin Sand, and Dr. Donald M. Dozer as prime examples. However, it seems that the Department of State has in recent years not availed itself of its best brains on this issue, relying instead upon mediocre, pusillanimous men displaying but one remarkable aptitude — a unique ability to compromise the United States and its vital interests. No Secretary of State has been willing to jettison American interests in the Panama Canal. But the faceless, nameless experts who have haunted every Secretary of State are always eager to do so.

Fortunately for our country, the Halls of Congress are filled with many men who are quite capable and ready to squash the rash moves of the ciphers of Foggy Bottom.

With the effect of political and diplomatic blunders associated with the 1967 proposed treaties neutralized, the time has arrived for a great decision. With any move to compromise the U.S. position blocked, we can now make perhaps the most momentous decision connected with the Panama Canal since our decision to build it.

The scene is now set for the final act. The script is prepared for the necessary, indeed vital, major improvement of the Panama Canal within the framework of our national rights and obligations. This script is the bill proposed by Senator Thurmond and Congressman Flood.

The plan proposed by these two distinguished and experienced legislators and national leaders will not only provide the best solution to the interoceanic canal problem at least cost but also will protect the economic interests of Panama as well as the United States. In addition, it best serves the users of the Panama Canal, of all nations, who have to pay tolls.

In this connection the reader should consider that U.S. public and private interests are the leading "customers" of the Canal. The Atlantic-Pacific Interoceanic Canal Study Commission has announced that it is evaluating the possibility of international financing of a new canal. Perhaps they have never heard that old saying, "He who pays the piper calls the tune."

The Atlantic-Pacific Interoceanic Study Commission has announced that their study concludes that all of the sea-level canals under consideration would enhance U.S. national security by decreased vulnerability and increased capacity. This conclusion, according to our most serious military experts and to our maritime industry can in no way be justified. Any canal — and for geological reasons especially a sea-level canal in Panama — would be vulnerable to nuclear attack. What experienced naval officer in a time of nuclear war would send ships through a death-trap such as a canal! As far as increased capacity is concerned, the Study Commission itself estimates that the present canal should be able to handle traffic as it presently estimates it to increase until 1985. Should the Terminal Lake-Third Locks Plan be undertaken, increased traffic should be easily handled in this century, and, with additional locks constructed as the need arises, should be easily handled indefinitely.

This same study commission has been very vague concerning possible costs of a sea-level canal, contending that final cost analysis will "await the development of Commission-approved data." The cost of a canal, as with any real estate venture, must include the costs of right of way and purchase of property and huge indemnities to Panama for the grant of the right to build such a canal. The Commission, unlike any sensible builder, has focused its attention almost entirely on construction problems. Considering the magnitude of construction problems in a sea-level canal project, one can hardly blame them, but, is this any way to run a canal? You bet it isn't.

This same commission seems to lack understanding that the battle for a "Two-Ocean Navy" was decided long ago and that the Navy's Ship's Characteristics Board has long since discarded requirements connected with Panama Canal considerations, e.g., size limited by locks. All far-seeing naval experts realize that nuclear capability (whether used or not) eliminates war-time usage of the Panama Canal in the event of a major conflagration involving the United States. Moreover, even current super-carriers, as the battle-ships before them, cannot be expected to maintain their strategic importance for a sufficient time to warrant their potential Panama Canal transit capability as a consideration for the twenty-first century.

This same commission infers that only a sea-level canal could handle the increased traffic and the larger ships projected in the growth of international maritime commerce. The present canal, if modernized under the Terminal Lake-Third Locks Plan, would be able to add a minimum of a 50% increase to present canal traffic. That would mean an increase from 26,000 to at least 39,000 transits per annum. With increased tandem transits and other planned improvements this could be increased even more.

The larger ships of such great concern to them — those presently unable to go through the canal because of their size — would be considerably fewer because of the increased width of the locks provided for by the Terminal Lake-Third Locks modernization plan. Those vessels which would still be too large to transit the canal were specifically designed so that they could make voyages on routes that would enable them to avoid the payment of any canal tolls as a part of their operating expenses.

The sea-level advocates never mention that, considering the low cost of providing water for additional lockages by pumping, the ultimate capacity of the Panama Canal with locks is unlimited. It may be increased to any amount needed by constructing additional locks and installing the necessary pumping equipment. This is something our merchant marine industry well understands. They cannot understand why the sea-level "experts" can't grasp it. Perhaps because it is too simple?

Those who would remove the United States from the Canal Zone allude to mythical private interests. What private interests? The Canal Zone is a United States Government reservation, as much so as Yellowstone National Park. There is no private property in the Canal Zone — American, Panamanian or any other. Every square foot is owned, through the U.S. Government, by the American taxpayer. No property is even leased to private interests, although essential businesses needed to provide services to Canal Zone personnel can hold temporary, revocable licenses. The real private interests to look out for are those firms which would make large profits out of the construction of an unnecessary new canal.

Construction of a sea-level canal would destroy the present "small boat channel" and "banana channel" which handle small craft mostly engaged in the internal economy of Panama. The resultant disruption of Panamanian commerce would subject the United States to the expense of justifiable indemnities, a point the sea-level advocates have not raised.

In conclusion, navigational factors, such as currents, tides, winds, fog, mist, heavy rain, hazards of restricted channels, machinery and steering gear failures which could cause the blocking of the channel, maneuvering characteristics, the use of tug boats, etc. should have the highest priority in evaluating the technical features of a canal.

The Terminal Lake-Third Lock Plan encompasses the best solutions to the navigational problems of Isthmian Canal passage between the Atlantic and Pacific Oceans.

Engineering factors, especially construction problems, must be evaluated very carefully. The Terminal Lake-Third Locks

Plan has been subject to extensive engineering study. It is far less difficult and far less expensive to accomplish than would be the construction of a sea-level canal.

And, as the advocates of a sea-level canal have not chosen to discuss, *there cannot be a true sea-level canal in the Isthmus*. No matter what type of construction would be utilized, tidal locks with many miles of high embankments on both sides for flood control purposes would be required. Ironically, they would be more complicated to operate than the present locks because they would have to serve for water flow in opposite directions.

Further, the United States paid for the present Canal Zone three times:

1) to Panama

2) to Colombia, of which Panama had been a part prior to 1903

3) to the private holders of property in the Canal Zone

We have ploughed over five billion dollars into the Panama Canal, and the Canal Zone represents our single most expensive territorial acquisition. The advocates of a sea-level canal would have us give up this investment and spend untold billions on a new canal we don't need.

On occasion there is an opportunity for the voice of the people to express themselves decisively. Now is such a time.
There is an urgent need for modernizing the Panama Canal. There is an urgent need to prevent the colossal waste which would be involved in building a new canal.

There is an urgent need to protect our sovereign rights over the Panama Canal.

It is that voice, in support of the bills providing for the Terminal Lake-Third Locks Plan introduced by Senator Strom Thurmond and Congressman Daniel J. Flood, which can make the difference. The President of the United States, the Members of the Senate, the Members of the House of Representatives, all respond to the reasoned voice of the people. Let that voice be heard.

APPENDIX A

Russia, America
and the Panama Canal

JON P. SPELLER

Jon P. Speller, Executive Editor of East Europe, *has been interested in Panama Canal matters for more than a decade. For the past two years he has been working on a book,* The Panama Canal: Heart of America's Security, *devoted to analysis supporting the major modernization of the Panama Canal proposed by Congressional Panama Canal experts Congressman Daniel Flood (Dem., Pa.) and Senator Strom Thurmond (Rep., S.C.).*

In recent years the Russians have vigorously entered into a race for naval supremacy over the United States. Except for the fact that they were foolish to throw down the gauntlet to a competitor with a superior geo-political and industrial base for seapower, the Russians have evidenced a high degree of professionalism in their strategic positioning. Many seapower analysts believe that Russia's naval strategists have placed a high priority on the objective of depriving the United States of use of the Panama Canal.

Recent months have disclosed construction activities essential for the establishment of a Russian submarine base at Cienfuegos, Cuba. A Soviet survey ship has been sighted at South Georgia in the South Atlantic, a potential site for a base controlling the eastern approaches to the only fully navigable passageway other than the Panama Canal connecting the Atlantic and Pacific Oceans in the Americas. The new regime in Chile, should it cooperate with the Russian Navy, could also provide bases suitable for control of the western approaches to these interoceanic straits.

Russian strategic planning related to the Southern Hemisphere is cause for alarm. But even more alarming is Russian strategic planning related to the Panama Canal.

The Panama Canal not only represents an essential maritime

link for our commerce, but, more importantly, an indispensable supply channel for our Armed Forces. The present locations of our Armed Forces heighten the importance of the Canal as related to our capability for flexible response.

Last September Moscow's *New Times* published an article entitled "New Trends in Panama" disclosing support for the government of General Torrijos in Panama. The views expressed in this Soviet publication are aimed at:

1) gaining international support for the Panamanian Government in its attempts to get control of the Canal;

2) a pretense of opposition to the proposed new Panamanian-American treaties in order to obfuscate the very real danger these treaties represent to the vital national interests of the United States.

The vital national interests of the United States — its defense from all enemies, present and potential — prescribe that we:

1) reaffirm our undiluted sovereignty over the Panama Canal Zone granted in perpetuity by Panama in the treaty of 1903;

2) increase security precautions related to the operation and maintenance of the canal in regard to the employment of aliens in security positions;

3) immediately proceed with major modernization of the existing canal.

Steps are now being taken on the Congress that aim to implement this program, which does not involve the negotiation of any new treaties with Panama and safeguards United States interests as well as the security of the entire Western Hemisphere, including Panama.

The *New Times* article, (September 30, 1970) attributed to Ruben Dario Souza, Russia's *sputnik* in Panama, is reproduced in full:

"Earlier this month the Panama government officially announced that the draft treaties on a new status for the Panama Canal, drawn up in Washington in 1967, were unacceptable as a basis for resuming negotiations on this question. The Panamanian authorities declared that the United States must turn over the Canal Zone to Panama.

"What prompted the Panamanian government's decision, which has come as a surprise to many? What are the roots of this turn in the country's foreign policy? *New Times* correspondent Juan Cobo put these questions to Ruben Dario Souza, General Secretary of the People's Party of Panama, who visited Moscow in September.

"At one time," Souza said, "press comment on developments in Panama was largely influenced by the fact that the National Guard, the only armed force in the country, which came to power after the coup of October 11, 1968, had been organized and trained by the Pentagon. Moreover, the Panamanian army leaders arrested a great many representatives of the opposition at the time. The Communists incidentally suffered most from the repressions. I myself was in prison until November last year.

"All this caused the world press to conclude that a conservative military dictatorship had taken over the reins of government. And to some extent, especially at that particular moment, this was indeed the case. However, as time went on, there were increasing signs that the ruling junta was by no means united, that a constant struggle was going on within it between the different views as to the direction the country's development should take.

"It is symptomatic that Washington was in no hurry to recognize the military regime. In the first place, the old order, under which the various clans of the corrupt pro-American oligarchy had alternated in government as a result of elections, suited the U.S. down to the ground. Secondly — and this is more important — the United States was informed by its intelligence agents of the existence of diverse tendencies among the Panama military, including progressive nationalist tendencies, and feared that the latter might take the upper hand. Washington evidently took into account the fact that the National Guard had been created only in 1953, that it was not a caste army, that it consisted of a large percentage of men from the lower and middle strata, who yearn for changes."

"How widespread are such sentiments in the Panama army at present?"

"Today after some reshuffling of the junta leadership, the nationalists are setting the tone. They are led by General Omar Torrijos, the actual leader of the junta and the commander-in-chief of the National Guard. The general described the evolution of his views in a letter to U.S. Senator Edward Kennedy which was published in July in the newspaper *Estrella de Panama*. Torrijos wrote that for a long time the Panama oligarchy had used him personally and the army generally for one purpose only — repressions against the people. This gradually opened his eyes to the cynicism of the former ruling elite and to the needs and demands of the popular masses. The same sort of evolution is taking place in the armed forces of many Latin American countries, and Torrijos attaches much significance to the emergence on the continent of a 'new type' of the military, to which he considers himself as belonging."

"Could the same not be said of the Peru military?"

"Certainly. More, some of Torrijos' colleagues, who have been clearing the country and the National Guard itself of CIA agents, studied at the Centre for Higher Military Studies in Lima and heard lectures by General Velasco Alvarado, now President of Peru. They speak of this with unconcealed pride and voice admiration for Peru's officers. Thus, the nationalist wing of the Panama army is influenced, not only by the sentiments of the Panamanian masses, but by the general shift to the Left in Latin America as manifested, among other things, in the present policy of the Peru military."

"In that case Washington's cautious attitude towards the Panamanian junta is indeed understandable . . ."

"Washington not only displayed caution, it did everything possible to get rid of Torrijos and his followers, whose position throughout last year grew steadily stronger. On December 15 four junta colonels took advantage of Torrijos' absence in being a Communist and allowing Leftists to penetrate the government. One of the conspirators, Colonel Sanjur, tried to induce the army officers to join in the putsch by assuring them over and over again that 'everything is in order; don't worry, the CIA guarantees us full support.' Official documents published after the conspiracy was exposed and Torrijos had regained control of the situation, charged the CIA with direct complicity in the putsch. And there is ample evidence to support the charge. Here is one fact. Three of the rebel colonels who escaped from jail shortly after their arrest were given asylum in the Zone and later, despite the protest of the Panamanian authorities, were sent on to the United States."

"What happened after that?"

"Judging by everything, the CIA-engineered putsch acted as a sort of catalyst of the processes that have long been maturing within the junta. It was this evidently that induced Torrijos and his group to take resolute action. And this was logical enough. Finding themselves in a political vacuum after the December 15 events, Torrijos and his followers appealed for support to the lower and middle sections of the population. And this naturally forced the army to give more attention to the aspirations of these sections.

"At the beginning of January this year Juan Antonio Tack, a man known for his progressive views, was appointed to the post of Foreign Minister. At a session of the Organization of American States, Tack delivered a speech denouncing imperialist policy.

"Certain changes have taken place in the internal life of Panama as well. This summer nearly all the political prisoners from progressive parties and organizations, including Communists, were released from jail. The government has recognized the National Labour Centre, formed this year as a counterweight to the old trade union confederation whose leadership was completely under the control of the Americans and the local oligarchies. Under pressure from the peasant masses, the agrarian reform has been speeded up. Student organizations, which have quite a revolutionary tradition in our country, have been restored.

"Then the Panamanian government's position on the question of the Canal may be seen as a logical manifestation of these new tendencies?

"Of course. But I should like to make it clear that Panamanians are concerned at present less about the question of the

Canal itself, than about the extensive zone which adjoins it and which has become a 'state within a state.' The Pentagon has turned the zone into a powerful base of operations located far south of the U.S. borders and spearheaded not only against Panama but against all of Latin America. That area should by rights belong to Panama—on this the bulk of the population of the country is unanimous.

"Now about the Canal itself and its exploitation. . . . Until quite recently there was a good deal of talk in Washington about the possibility of building a new waterway between the Atlantic and the Pacific, a sea-level canal cutting across Panama, Colombia or Nicaragua, big enough to accommodate modern vessels. But of the 25 million dollars allocated by the U.S. Congress for surveying the new routes, $18 million were earmarked for work in Panama. And not long ago it transpired that the Americans had decided simply to expand and reconstruct the existing canal. In violation of all legal norms, they proceeded to put their project in operation without even informing the Panamanian authorities of their intention. The Panama government protested the action and the National Guard occupied the neighboring Rio Hato area, formerly a Pentagon artillery range.

"After that the draft treaties on a new status for the Canal, drawn up to the detriment of our country's interests back in 1967, were in effect declared invalid by Torrijos. It was at this point that the *Christian Science Monitor* wrote about Washington's concern over indications of General Torrijos 'wanting to follow a more independent, nationalistic course.'"

"What was the reaction of the Panamanian democrats to this?"

"The Left forces, and particularly the Communists, regard the present developments as positive. The Panamanian democrats do not close their eyes to the fact that the policy of the Torrijos government is a variety of bourgeois reformism, that in many respects it is dictated by objective circumstances and is none too firm. Nevertheless, we are convinced that in the interests of the democratic forces we must make use of the specific nature of the present period which we regard as transitional.

"The principal task, the Communists hold, is to build an alliance of all the anti-imperialist forces in Panama and secure the establishment of a truly democratic system which would make it possible to intensify the struggle for genuine independence. We fully realize that this is by no means an easy task. Washington will of course continue to seek allies in the armed forces in order to achieve its ends with their help. If it fails, it is not excluded that the CIA will try to build up reactionary terrorist organizations and sow havoc in the country, as it did in Guatemala. All the more important is it for us to strengthen the unity of all anti-imperialist forces and together counter the machinations of Yankee imperialism."

APPENDIX B

New Russian Tactics
on the Panama Canal

Moscow's *sputnik* in Panama, Ruben Dario Sousa, has followed up his propaganda campaign with a lengthy article in the February, 1971 *World Marxist Review*. In his article, "Panama: New Developments", Sr. Dario Sousa continued to heap praise on Panama's ruling junta and, of course, on "the growing might of the Soviet Union."

In his call for "progressives" throughout the world to give further support to the little clique of adventurers running Panama today, Dario Sousa says that "the national democratic (*sic,* ed.) revolution is one way of doing this (progress?, ed.) as far as Latin America is concerned. Its purpose is to establish a government representing diverse classes with the exception of the big monopolistic, pro-U.S. bourgeoisie." When was the oligarchy in Panama "pro-U.S.", Sr. Dario Sousa? We have trouble enough with our own "monopolists" and certainly don't need yours.

Sr. Dario Sousa praises the junta's foreign policy: "Things began to change also in foreign policy. The Panamanian representatives trenchantly criticized the Organization of American States at one of its conferences and the government rejected a U.S. proposal to prolong the lease of the Rio-Hàto air base, which expired last August, and Washington's draft treaties on the Panama Canal, military cooperation and construction of a new canal as an unacceptable basis for negotiation."

Please, Sr. Dario Sousa. Your Foreign Minister Tack has informed you that the government of Panama had issued an invitation to visit Panama to Robert B. Anderson, architect of the discredited 1967 draft treaties and leading proponent of the economically ridiculous and militarily unnecessary sea-level canal. Mr. Anderson's trip was to serve, according to the Panama Star & Herald (March 30, 1971), "as a prelude to a formal announcement by the two countries of the resumption of Panama Canal Treaty negotiations."

In praising the junta for "rejecting" these treaties—part of his justification for support of the junta—Sr. Dario Sousa neglected to mention that one of the most active supporters of these treaties in the United States, Daniel Hofgren, is presently employed by Goldman Sachs, financial representative in the United States for the government of Panama—Sr. Dario Sousa's favorite junta. Mr. Hofgren recently joined this firm after leaving his position as a Special Assistant in the White House with the personal rank of Ambassador while negotiating for the U.S. with Panama.

It is no secret that these draft treaties were dropped like a "hot potato" in 1967 when patriotic Senators and Congressmen, led by Senator Strom Thurmond and Congressman Daniel Flood, raised the ire of the American people against the possible jettisoning of a key to our national security—the operation, maintenance and defense of the Panama Canal under U.S. sovereignty. That the wrath came from both Democrats and Republicans, conservatives and liberals, did not escape the eyes of Sr. Dario Sousa's bosses in Moscow.

We are well aware of Russia's strategic designs on the

Panama Canal and the dangers the proposed treaties pose—the undermining of U.S. national security. The new tactics of Moscow—a pretense of opposition to the treaties—will have no more success than their old tactics had.

That Moscow's policy in regard to the Panama Canal is dictated by Soviet military and naval strategists is abundantly clear. As Senator Strom Thurmond has said:

"Vessels in the Soviet Navy are relatively new while many U.S. vessels are over age. Russia has a total of 1,500 naval vessels in commission whereas the United States has about 550 vessels. In range and firepower most new Soviet naval vessels outmatch ours and have a 1-to-3 knot superiority in speed. The Soviet Navy is superior to ours in submarines. The United States is superior in giant aircraft carriers, but these are a 'wasting asset' which someday will be superseded. The Soviets are preparing to "leapfrog" the carrier stage of naval development. Unless the United States strengthens our Navy rapidly the Soviets will be in a position to challenge us successfully on the high seas; and it has already conducted global naval maneuvers—something the United States has never attempted."

Admiral Gorshkov and the Russian Fleet are aware of Admiral Mahan's description of the strategic importance of the Panama Canal area to America's security: ". . . the exclusion of direct European political control from the Isthmus of Panama is really as much a matter of national defense as is the protection of New York Harbor."[1]

But many Americans are equally aware of these truths.

---

[1] Lessons of the War with Spain by Alfred T. Mahan, Boston: Little, Brown, 1899, p. 298.

BIBLIOGRAPHY

Bradley, Hon. Willis W.: "What of the Panama Canal?" *Congressional Record* (80th Cong., 2d Sess.), Vol. 94, Pt. 10 (Apr. 21, 1948), pp A2449-53.

Briggs, Prof. John C.: "The Sea-Level Panama Canal: Potential Biological Catastrophe." *Bio Science* (Washington, D.C.), Vol. 19 (Jan. 1969), pp. 44-47.

Dozer, Dr. Donald M.: "The Interoceanic Canal Problem in the Americas." *Latin America: Politics, Economics, and Hemispheric Security*. Ed., Norman A. Bailey. New York: Frederick A. Praeger, Publishers, 1965, pp. 51-78.

Duncan, Hon. John J.: "Future Ownership and Operation of the Panama Canal." *Congressional Record* (90th Cong., 1st Sess.), Vol. 113, Pt. 17 (Aug. 15, 1967), pp. 22710-12.

DuVal, Captain Miles P., Jr.: *Cadiz to Cathay*. (3rd Edition). New York: Greenwood Press, 1968.
_____.: *And the Mountains Will Move*. Stanford, Calif.: Stanford University Press, 1947. 2nd ed. New York and West-port, Conn.: Greenwood Press, 1969.
_____.: "The Marine Operating Problems, Panama Canal, and the Solution." American Society of Civil Engineers, *Transactions* (New York, N.Y.), Vol. 114 (1949), pp. 558-71.
_____.: "Isthmian Canal Policy — An Evaluation." U.S. Naval Institute *Proceedings* (Annapolis, Md.), Vol. 81 (Mar. 1955), pp. 263-75.

_____.: "Panama Canal." *Encyclopaedia Britannica* (Chicago), Vol. 17 (1969), pp. 205-12.

Edgerton, Gov. Glen E.: "Report on Proposals for the Elimination of Pedro Miguel Locks of the Panama Canal." *Congressional Record* (84th Cong., 1st Sess.), Vol. 102, Pt. 8 (June 21, 1956), pp. 10756-66.

Flood, Hon. Daniel J.: "Isthmian Canal Policy Questions: List of Representative Flood's Contributions." *Congressional Record* (91st Cong., 1st Sess.), Vol. 115, No. 73 (May 6, 1969), pp. 43411-14 (Temp.)
_____.: *Isthmian Canal Policy Questions* (Ho. Doc. No. 474, 89th Congress, 2d Session). Washington: U.S. Government Printing Office, 1966.

Harding, Earl; *The Untold Story of Panama*. New York: Athene Press, 1959.

Hepburn, Admiral A.J.: "Panama Canal: Report of the Chairman of the General Board of the Navy to the Secretary of the Navy, Sept. 30, 1943. *Congressional Record* (85th Cong., 1st Sess.), Vol. 103, Pt. 12 (Aug. 12, 1957), pp. 16504-06.

Randolph, E. Sydney: "An Engineer's Evaluation of Isthmian Canal Policy." U.S. Naval Institute *Proceedings* (Annapolis, Md.), Vol. 82 (April 1956), pp. 395-99.

Rarick, Hon. John R.: "Panama Canal: Giveaway By Treaty Must Be Prevented." *Congressional Record* (90th Cong., 1st Sess.), Vol. 113, Pt. 10 (May 22, 1967), pp. 13391-94.

Settle, Vice Admiral T.G.W. and Dr. Donald M. Dozer: *Panama Canal Issues and Treaty Talks — Minority Report*. Washington, D.C.: Center for Strategic Studies, Georgetown University, 1967, pp. 69-83.

Stratton, Col. James H. et al.: "Panama Canal-Sea-Level Project Symposium." American Society of Civil Engineers *Transactions* (New York), Vol. 114 (1949), pp. 607-906.

Thompson, Hon. Clark W.: "Isthmian Canal Policy of the United States — Documentation." *Congressional Record* (84th Cong., 1st Sess.), Vol. 101, Pt. 3 (Mar. 23, 1955), pp. 3610-16.

Thurmond, Hon. Strom: "Bibliography of Panama Canal Issues." *Congressional Record* (90th Cong., 1st Sess.), Vol. 113, No. 105 (July 10, 1967), pp.
_____.: "Hand List of Panama Canal Treaty Statements." *Congressional Record* (90th Cong., 1st Sess.), Vol. 113, Pt. 17 (Aug. 15, 1967), 22622.

THE TERMINAL LAKE-THIRD LOCKS
PLAN FOR IMPROVEMENT
OF
THE PANAMA CANAL

The elimination of the bottleneck Pedro Miguel locks, raising of the level of Miraflores Lake, and consolidation of the Pacific locks.

INDEX